Penguin Critical Studies

Wuthering Heights

Dr Rod Mengham is a Temporary Lecturer in the Faculty of English at Cambridge and a Fellow of Gonville and Caius College. He was educated at the Universities of Cambridge and Edinburgh and has taught in schools and universities in England and Poland. Previous publications include *The Idiom of the Time: The Writings of Henry Green* (Cambridge University Press, 1982). He is now at work on a study of contemporary poetic writing.

Penguin Critical Studies
Advisory Editors:
Stephen Cooke and Bryan Loughrey

Emily Brontë

Wuthering Heights

Rod Mengham

Penguin Books

PENGUIN BOOKS

Published by the Penguin Group
27 Wrights Lane, London W8 5TZ, England
Viking Penguin Inc., 40 West 23rd Street, New York, New York 10010, USA
Penguin Books Australia Ltd, Ringwood, Victoria, Australia
Penguin Books Canada Ltd, 2801 John Street, Markham, Ontario, Canada L3R 1B4
Penguin Books (NZ) Ltd, 182–190 Wairau Road, Auckland 10, New Zealand

Penguin Books Ltd, Registered Offices: Harmondsworth, Middlesex, England

First published 1989

Made and printed in Great Britain by
Richard Clay Ltd, Bungay, Suffolk

Filmset in 9pt Monophoto Times

Contents

Preface

Although this study is in the main part a close reading of the text of *Wuthering Heights*, it starts off with a brief review of the life and times of its author. No one is likely to want to dispute the relevance of biographical material to any critical account of the novel which aims to be thorough. However, it may be thought unnecessary to go over old ground, even when the ground in question is coextensive with that of the Yorkshire moors near Haworth. My object in adopting a 'background' approach in the first three chapters is to unsettle the emphases which are usually placed on certain aspects of Emily Brontë's upbringing. I want to shift attention away from the sensational nature of much of her life in order to enlarge the significance of her social position as member of a particular family and of a particular community. Because this might be said to need a lot of proving, I have split the material into three parts, so that a single career can be observed through a gradually widening focus. In this way, the reader can see the adjustments taking place and is given advance warning of them.

The first chapter is accordingly a plain summary of the events of Brontë's life. For those who already know the story, there is no need to read it in this version. But for those who want to be told what actually happened to Emily Brontë, the intention is to provide them with the raw material before it is handled critically. The second and third chapters place a construction on the bare facts which is meant to contribute to the overall coherence of my reading of the novel. Chapter 2 examines the Brontë family, considering it as a tightly knit social unit exclusive of others but inwardly strained by massive tensions of a social, political and religious order as well as by personal antagonisms. The angle of approach may give a useful insight into the strangely parallel pressures for dependence and independence in the novel. Chapter 3 looks at Haworth as something more than just a point of access to the moors. Social change and political agitation were marked and on the increase in this very part of Yorkshire throughout the entirety of Brontë's life. It is not only in the violent moods of a great deal of her writing but in the language and structure of her novel that she tackles the problems of destructive conflict between groups of people and of divided loyalties and confusions of purpose within individuals. I am fully persuaded of the need to read *Wuthering*

Heights in the context of local industrialization, and hope to persuade others.

One technical point: every critic of this novel is exercised by the need to distinguish between the two heroines bearing the same name. There is no ideal solution of this problem, which I have tried to overcome by naming the elder character Cathy and the younger one Catherine, occasionally reinforcing the distinction with a reference to 'the younger Catherine'. This is apt to occasion awkwardness, which I hope the reader will put up with for the sake of accuracy.

All page references to *Wuthering Heights* are to the Penguin English Library edition edited by David Daiches (Penguin Books, 1965, reissued in Penguin Classics, 1985).

1. Emily Brontë

When Emily Brontë was born, on 30 July 1818, she was the fifth child in a family whose eldest child was only four years three months old. The father, Patrick Brontë, was then parson at Thornton near Bradford, but shortly after the birth of Emily's younger sister, Anne, in 1820, the family moved eight miles away to Haworth, where Patrick was to be 'perpetual curate'; the parsonage was to remain home for Emily for the rest of her life.

The fresh start at Haworth soon turned sour with the death of the mother, aged thirty-eight, from cancer. What this meant to the children, apart from bewilderment, was the arrival of their aunt to keep house. Elizabeth Branwell found Haworth much less civilized than her native Penzance and was never wholly reconciled to it. She was always unpopular with the daughters of the house, who were later to recognize only that she had taught them the meaning of duty, order and punctuality.

Of Emily as a small child little is known, except that the servants thought her the prettiest of the children. She was already noted for her secrecy of manner, a trait that was to be more and more remarked upon as the years went by. Characteristic also was a lack of compromise, evident in her reply to her father's question 'what I had best to do with her brother Branwell, who was sometimes a naughty boy'. 'Reason with him,' reasoned the six-year-old Emily, 'and when he won't listen to reason, whip him.'[1]

The great event of her early life was going away to school. This was the notorious Clergy Daughters' School at Cowan Bridge, which killed off her elder sisters Maria and Elizabeth, and which affected Charlotte strongly enough to provide the basis of the most pathetic episodes in her novel *Jane Eyre*, written over twenty years later. Emily was the youngest pupil at the school, and appears to have been petted by both staff and pupils alike. She remained there a little over six months before being rescued by her father.

The return home began a period under the influence of her mercurial brother Branwell. The wildness of his imagination was such that he claimed to hear the voice of Maria outside the windows at night (a circumstance perhaps to be noted by the reader of *Wuthering Heights*). It was during this time when the three sisters and brother were all at

1

home that they began to invent an imaginary world of their own. It started with a box of toys:

Papa bought Branwell some wooden soldiers at Leeds. When Papa came home it was night, and we were in bed, so next morning Branwell came to our door with a box of soldiers. Emily and I jumped out of bed, and I snatched up one and exclaimed: 'This is the Duke of Wellington! This shall be the Duke!' When I had said this Emily likewise took up one and said it should be hers; when Anne came down, she said one should be hers. Mine was the prettiest of the whole, and the tallest, and the most perfect in every part. Emily's was a grave-looking fellow, and we called him 'Gravey'. Anne's was a queer little thing, much like herself, and we called him 'Waiting-Boy'. Branwell chose his, and called him Buonaparte.[2]

According to Branwell, Emily's soldier was not called 'Gravey' at first but 'Parry' after the arctic explorer Captain Edward Parry. Certainly, Parry is the name that crops up time and again in the chronicles, poems, narratives and plays that began to be produced. Its adoption by Emily says something of the importance to her both of stark landscapes and of strength of purpose. Her close attachment to the Yorkshire moors has always been reckoned a chief element in her character, while the intrepidity of an explorer was almost the first quality attributed to her by M. Heger, who taught her in Brussels in 1842: 'She should have been a man – a great navigator,' he said.

The imaginary world was called 'Glasstown', then renamed 'Angria'. For a while, Emily and Anne were too young to make anything more than verbal contributions, but when they were ready to strike out on their own they created a separate world called 'Gondal'. It did not reproduce the features of 'Angria'. For a start, its major character was a defiant woman, and its predominant mood, perhaps, was one of endurance in the face of oppression.

These earliest writings were highly literary. The children were avid readers of their father's library, which held works of history, biography and poetry (especially the complete works of Milton and Byron). They could also borrow books from the Keighley Mechanics' Institute Library, of which their father was a founding member. But the biggest impact of any book on Emily seems to have been *Tales of a Grandfather* by Sir Walter Scott, given by Aunt Branwell as a New Year's present in 1828. The Gondal landscape was formed as a Scottish one – when it was not a West Riding one – and most of the Gondal heroes were given Scottish names. Apart from Scott, and the Gothic stories of *Blackwood's Magazine*, the family did not read much fiction.

Emily's reading does show in her work, but it is easy to pay too much attention to literary influences. Sister Charlotte said as much in 1850 to the then readers of *Wuthering Heights*:

Neither Emily nor Anne was learned; they had no thought of filling their pitchers at the well-spring of other minds; they always wrote from the impulse of nature, the dictates of intuition, and from such stores of observation as their limited experience had enabled them to amass.[3]

Of equal importance to Emily was the oral transmission of local stories and sung ballads, and the key figure in this respect was the family servant Tabitha Aykroyd, known to the children as 'Tabby'. She came to the parsonage as a widow, already in her late fifties. Devoted to all the children, she was particularly attentive to Emily, and critics have often seen her as a prototype for Nelly Dean, the chief narrator of *Wuthering Heights*, even though she was simpler and less ambitious than her fictional counterpart. What she does share with Nelly is a store of local knowledge going back beyond the time in which the novel is set; certain of Tabby's stories seem to have been echoed in the circumstances of *Wuthering Heights*.

We have some record of Emily as a teenager in the account of Charlotte's close friend, Ellen Nussey. She remembered primarily her intense reserve, which seemed to be deepening with the years, her love of nature and her love of animals: she liked nothing better than walking her dogs on the moors above Haworth. Ellen's observations can be trusted not only to the extent of her devotion to the Brontë family, but also because Emily seems to have warmed a little towards her. On one occasion she amazed the whole family by offering to accompany Ellen on a walk because Charlotte was too ill to go. Interestingly, Ellen found her relatively forthcoming in the kind of mood she was to develop in *Wuthering Heights*:

Emily, half reclining on a slab of stone, played like a young child with the tadpoles in the water, making them swim about, and then fell to moralizing on the strong and the weak, the brave and the cowardly, as she chased them with her hand.[4]

Physically, she had grown into the tallest person in the house except her father. Her tightly curled hair was thought to be 'unbecoming', unlike her grey-blue eyes which were beautiful but rarely seen. Intimates were not the only ones to wonder at the degree of her withdrawal into herself. The villagers noticed how she turned her gaze away from them and preferred not to speak. And it was a matter for gossip that a parson's daughter refused to teach in the Sunday School and seldom even went to church. Emily's indifference to established religion was constant and only grew stronger. The single comment her sister Charlotte remembered her to have made on religion was a brusque 'That's right', in support of the opinion that religion was a private matter between God and oneself.

Surprisingly, there is almost as little personal documentation of the adult Emily as there is of the child. Only three short letters from her have survived. Perhaps the most revealing evidence is that of the diary papers she wrote once every four years in association with Anne. These compositions were meant to reflect on the girls' present state and to speculate about the future. The first and possibly the most famous of them was written when Emily was already sixteen years old:

> November the 24 1834 Monday
> Emily Jane Bronte
> Anne Bronte

I fed Rainbow, Diamond Snowflake Jasper phaesant (alias) this morning Branwell went down to Mr. Driver's and brought news that Sir Robert Peel was going to be invited to stand for Leeds Anne and I have been peeling apples for Charlotte to make us an apple pudding and for Aunt nuts and apples Charlotte said she made puddings perfectly and she was of a quick but limited intellect. Taby said just now Come Anne pilloputate [i.e. pill a potato] Aunt has come into the kitchen just now and said where are your feet Anne Anne answered On the floor Aunt papa opened the parlour door and gave Branwell a letter saying here Branwell read this and show it to your Aunt and Charlotte – The Gondals are discovering the interior of Gaaldine Sally Mosley is washing in the back kitchen [5]

What this unpremeditated chatter reveals is a mind in which the worlds of fantasy, domesticity and public affairs are as one. Gondal is as much a part of everyday life as peeling potatoes or waiting for the Parliamentary news. Nothing shows more effectively how natural it was for Emily Brontë to be immersed in a world of her own making.

Her main pursuits, apart from helping in the house, were essentially solitary ones: wandering on the moors, writing, drawing and playing the piano. She was a capable artist, as her surviving drawings (characteristically of animals) prove, and an outstanding pianist. Ellen Nussey was full of praise for her musical abilities and later on in Brussels the Hegers thought it necessary to send her for lessons with the finest teacher in Belgium. (Their intentions were never realized.)

Given her increasing dependence on her private world, and her need for solitude, it is not surprising that her next experiment with school life as a pupil was a complete disaster. Having been at home for ten years, she left for Roe Head on the eve of her seventeenth birthday. She found she could not stand the meaningless regimentation and the learning by rote and quickly fell ill of homesickness. She could not eat properly, nor sleep, and when Charlotte said she was sure she would die, Emily was sent home – after only three months.

Her failure to adapt to a new pattern of life would have made her doubly sympathetic to Branwell, who had just come home in disgrace, having squandered his only chance of joining the Royal Academy Schools in London. The two were largely confined to each other's company for the next two years while Charlotte and Anne were away at school. Emily would have understood Branwell's experience as a misfit but she did not share his complete inability to lead an ordinary life. In fact, she was well known to the others as the most practical member of the family. When Tabby broke her leg, just before Christmas 1836, it was Emily who replaced her as housekeeper and who made a success of the task. She came to be respected locally for her bread-making, although she performed this chore with a book and paper and pencil ready on the table where she kneaded the dough. Years later, when there were plans for the sisters to establish a school of their own, Charlotte foresaw Emily less in the role of teacher than of housekeeper, and she knew she could rely on her sister's help in comforting the smaller and lonelier girls. Anne was to write in her diary paper of 1841:

We are now all separate and not likely to meet again for many a weary week, but we are none of us ill that I know of and all are doing something for our own livelihood except Emily, who, however, is as busy as any of us, and in reality earns her food and raiment as much as we do.[6]

But if Charlotte and Anne could justify her usefulness, Emily must have had trouble in doing so herself once Tabby's leg had healed and Branwell had left to be usher in a boys' school at Halifax. In 1837 she took steps to earn her own living, as a teacher at Law Hill, also near Halifax. Of course, the attempt was ill-fated. Charlotte reported to Ellen Nussey that Emily had to work from six in the morning until eleven at night, with only half an hour of exercise in between. There are conflicting views on the length of her stay, but in any event it was no less than six months and no more than eighteen. The state of her mind can be judged from the fact that she once told a classroom of girls that the only being she liked in the place was the house dog. Of course, to anyone who knew her, this preference for animals would have come as no surprise, and it was owing to her influence that the household in the parsonage later expanded to include not only dogs and cats, but tame geese and a hawk.

Clearly, the Law Hill experience felt like a wholly negative one, but it may have been productive in some ways; if we look at what was incidental rather than essential to her life there, we find that one of the members of staff was a woman called Earnshaw and that the nearby High Sunderland Hall had carvings round its door with the date set over it just like the farmhouse at Wuthering Heights. Even more remarkable was the story of Law Hill itself, and of its founder Jack Sharp. Sharp had been adopted into the wealthy Walker family of Walterclough Hall barely a mile away. Far from showing his gratitude for this benevolence, he proceeded to ruin the family, to degrade several members of it, and to plot revenge against those who tried to stand in his way. If any of these circumstances made a difference to the shaping of *Wuthering Heights*, it is just as likely that conditions at home lent themselves to the atmosphere of the book. Branwell was becoming a permanent liability; he threw up the job as usher and tried unsuccessfully to become a portrait painter in Bradford. When he returned heavily in debt, it was to get frequently drunk and to start a long addiction to opium. Emily bore the brunt of coping with him, since Charlotte and Anne were working elsewhere as governesses. If she could not escape the daily spectacle of her brother's depravity, neither was she unaware of what was also found objectionable when presented in *Wuthering Heights* – the supernatural. Her father's curate lived in haunted lodgings. When Branwell spent the night in them, hoping to win a bet, he ended up running screaming from the house. As Winifred Gérin claimed, in her biography of the writer, 'Emily's contact with the world through her father and brother, the parish sexton, and the servants, provided a richer vicarious experience than Emily's sisters could enjoy in their cloistered schools and employments.' [7]

In one other way, Branwell's behaviour at this time reminds us of a part of *Wuthering Heights*. During the summer of 1840, Mary Taylor, a schoolfriend of Charlotte's, visited the parsonage. She had once been beloved of Branwell, but when she now showed signs of returning his feelings, he beat a retreat. Charlotte gave a wry account of it in a letter to Ellen Nussey. What it recalls is the beginning of the book and something that happens – not to Heathcliff, this time – but to Lockwood.

While Emily was always unhappy when displaced from home, it seems to have been the case that Charlotte and Anne were also less than satisfied with their respective posts as governesses. They hit on a plan which would solve all their problems, that of starting a school of their own. Emily went along with this, probably out of a sense of duty towards her sisters rather than from a real enthusiasm of her own. Charlotte was advised that in order to attract pupils they must be able to offer foreign languages on the curriculum. And so it was decided that she and Emily would spend a year in Brussels improving their French.

Nothing could be more in character for Charlotte, and less in character for Emily. It changed the life of the first, and coloured everything she wrote, but if you look in Emily's writings for any trace of her stay on the continent, she might just as well have never been. The school at least was an improvement on English establishments; it was liberal, and comfortable, and Emily made good use of her time. She did not see eye to eye with her teacher of French, M. Heger (she criticized his teaching methods to his face) but she reached a high level in her mastery of the language. Heger possessed a foul temper, but he was a very perceptive man and his is one of the shrewdest estimates of Emily's character and abilities:

Emily had a head for logic, and a capability of argument, unusual in a man, and rare indeed in a woman . . . Impairing the force of this gift, was her stubborn tenacity of will, which rendered her obtuse to all reasoning where her own wishes, or her own sense of right, was concerned . . . her strong imperious will would never have been daunted by opposition or difficulty; never have given way but with life. And yet, moreover, her faculty of imagination was such that, if she had written a history, her view of scenes and characters would have been so vivid, and so powerfully expressed, and supported by such a show of argument, that it would have dominated over the reader, whatever might have been his previous opinions, or his cooler perceptions of its truth.[8]

She did not manage to endear herself to many of the other pupils, who remembered her later as clinging fiercely to Charlotte. Obviously, the usual strains were all there, off-set this time by the constant presence of her sister. It was her longest absence from Haworth, and it might have been much longer but for the death of her aunt in October 1842. Her nieces were surprised to discover that Elizabeth Branwell had left them £350 apiece in her will. What this gave to Emily was a modicum of independence; she could now afford to do what she most wanted to do and live once more within walking distance of the Haworth moors.

After Christmas, Charlotte returned to Brussels, while Anne and Branwell went to work as teachers for the same employer, Mr Robinson of Thorp Green. It was Branwell's last chance; he had been dismissed from his previous post as railway clerk on suspicion of conniving at embezzlement. Emily was left in complete control of the house, and her first act was to reinstate Tabby on a permanent basis. However, Tabby was well advanced in years, and Emily had to take upon herself all of the cooking, baking, ironing and most of the housework.

She also had to spend increasing amounts of time reading to her father, whose sight was failing drastically. In the closeness that they inevitably developed, Mr Brontë came to regard Emily as something like the son Branwell had failed to be. He taught her how to shoot, so that she could protect the house in the event of marauders – a possibility he genuinely believed in. The family as a whole was ready to accord her a similarly masculine kind of toughness; there was the incident when, having been bitten by a mad dog, she rushed straight into the kitchen and unblinkingly cauterized the wound herself with one of Tabby's 'red-hot Italian irons'.

If the two-year period after her aunt's death kept her physically busy, it was also a phase of energetic creativity. In the New Year 1844 she started collecting her poems into two separate notebooks, one entitled 'Gondal Poems' and the other containing poems of a supposedly more 'personal' nature. The year 1844 was perhaps the Brontë family's most climactic year. Charlotte arrived home a nervous wreck after the disaster of having declared her passion to M. Heger; and Branwell received his final dismissal on the grounds of seducing his employer's wife. He was genuinely in love with her, and to be parted from her nearly killed him. He immediately suffered eleven nights without sleep which made him nearly blind, followed by nine weeks of complete mental and physical breakdown. It was Emily to whom Charlotte turned and whom Branwell could rely on not to judge him.

During the period of her extended recovery, Charlotte made the discovery that was to launch the Brontës into print:

One day, in the autumn of 1845, I accidentally lighted on a MS. volume of verse in my sister Emily's handwriting. Of course, I was not surprised, knowing that she could and did write verse: I looked it over, and something more than surprise seized me, – a deep conviction that these were not common effusions, not at all like the poetry women generally write. I thought them condensed and terse, vigorous and genuine. To my ear, they had also a peculiar music – wild, melancholy, and elevating.

My sister Emily was not a person of demonstrative character, nor one, on the recesses of whose mind and feelings, even those nearest and dearest to her could, with impunity, intrude unlicensed; it took hours to reconcile her to the discovery I had made, and days to persuade her that such poems merited publication. I knew, however, that a mind like hers could not be without some latent spark of honourable ambition, and refused to be discouraged in my attempts to fan that spark to flame.[9]

Quite simply, Emily was furious with her sister for intruding on her private world and never really overcame the reluctance to share it that is suggested by the force of that initial outburst. One suspects that Charlotte would have to play on more than ambition – on sisterly loyalty, perhaps – in order to ensure the publication of a joint volume including poems by all three sisters. In the event, the volume appeared at the Brontës' own expense under the title of *Poems* with the masculine (but not completely masculine) sounding pseudonyms of Currer, Ellis and Acton Bell.

Emily was much more reconciled to the idea of publishing the novel she now worked hard at. After *Poems* had failed to sell more than two copies, the sisters realized that their only hope of commercial success lay in fiction. The major part of the composition of *Wuthering Heights* was accomplished between the autumns of 1845 and 1846, when the family was in its worst ever state. Branwell's former employer had died, but instead of the expected reunion, Branwell was devastated to learn that a codicil to the will prevented him from seeing the wife on pain of her disinheritance. He was not to know that the codicil was an invention of the wife herself, whose callous treatment of Branwell effectively killed him. From this point on he behaved in an insane fashion, carrying around a carving knife in the expectation of meeting Satan, setting fire to his bed, and starving himself to such a degree that shortly before his death the neighbours were laughing at him for wearing his father's coat; it was in fact his own coat but he had become grotesquely thin. Throughout this final episode Charlotte would not even speak to him, while Emily did all she could for her brother, who was being literally torn apart by the disappointment of his love. Her goodness to Branwell was talked about in Haworth for a long time after the Brontës were all dead.

The novel was finished and sent out with Charlotte's *The Professor* and Anne's *Agnes Grey* in the hope that together they would comprise the required three-decker. They were disappointed by many publishers before Anne and Emily were accepted by Thomas Newby, who was to turn out such a disaster. Charlotte was much luckier with Smith, Elder & Co, who were more scrupulous, offered better terms, and who managed to publish her second novel, *Jane Eyre*, months before the appearance of *Agnes Grey* and *Wuthering Heights*. When these two novels finally did see the light of day, in December 1847, they were full of mistakes because Newby had ignored the authors' corrections to the proof sheets. Moreover, he deliberately tried to confuse the identities of the 'Bell brothers' in order to exploit the runaway success of *Jane Eyre*.

As if this wasn't enough, when the reviews came out, *Wuthering Heights* met with almost universal hostility; as a rule, Emily was indifferent to praise or blame, but she cannot have been completely immune to the wholeheartedness of some of the attacks. The final blow in her unfortunate experience of publishing came when Charlotte and Anne revealed the true authorship of the novels so as to prevent the spread of further confusion. From first to last, Emily had placed a high value on the privacy afforded her by a pseudonym, and with its loss she turned on Charlotte with an indignation almost equal to the resentment shown at her sister's first discovery of her poems. From this point on she seemed not to trust Charlotte; she ignored her actually very sound advice to change publishers and stubbornly entered into negotiations with Newby on the terms for a second novel. The second novel came to nothing; while her sisters planned and wrote their next books, Emily fell silent. Part of her reason for withdrawing from the whole business of writing and publishing may have been a grudge that Branwell had not been included in any of the family projects.

It was during this period of bitter disillusionment that Branwell died. Charlotte reacted with an attack of jaundice but gradually regained her strength. Emily stood firm in the immediate aftermath of the event and then went into a decline from which she never recovered. The villagers were later quite sure that she had died of grief for her brother. This is far too simple a view, but it seems important to remember that her only previous serious illness, at Roe Head, had been psychosomatically induced. Branwell's funeral service was the last time she went out. She caught a cold at the graveside but instead of attempting to cure it she systematically neglected every means of safeguarding her health. She would neither rest nor consult a doctor, and she simply became less and less responsive to the appeals of her sisters – only a month after Branwell's death she would not even speak when spoken to. Her symptoms were emaciation, breathlessness, an extremely high pulse rate and a worsening cough, and yet she persisted in carrying out all her usual household tasks. On the very morning that she died she got up and got dressed, even with the death rattle in her throat. Her last words – 'If you'll send for a doctor I'll see him now' – were probably uttered to allay her sisters' distress. When she died, on 19 December 1848, her favourite dog, Keeper, set up a cry outside the bedroom door that reportedly lasted for weeks. At the funeral it was Keeper, along with Mr Brontë himself, who headed the procession.

Charlotte seemed never to fully recover from the shocking experience of watching Emily kill herself. When she later compared her death with that of Anne (who succumbed to tuberculosis barely five months later) she laid so much stress on the Christian nature of Anne's passing that it only helped to suggest how very un-Christian Emily's had been:

Never in all her life had she lingered over any task that lay before her, and she did not linger now. She sank rapidly. She made haste to leave us. Yet, while physically she perished, mentally, she grew stronger than we had yet known her. Day by day, when I saw with what a front she met suffering, I looked on her with an anguish of wonder and love. I have seen nothing like it; but, indeed, I have never seen her parallel in anything. Stronger than a man, simpler than a child, her nature stood alone. The awful point was, that, while full of ruth for others, on herself she had no pity; the spirit was inexorable to the flesh; from the trembling hand, the unnerved limbs, the faded eyes, the same service was exacted as they had rendered in health. To stand by and witness this, and not dare to remonstrate, was a pain no words can render.

Two cruel months of hope and fear passed painfully by, and the day came at last when the terrors and pains of death were to be undergone by this treasure, which had grown dearer and dearer to our hearts as it wasted before our eyes. Towards the decline of that day, we had nothing left of Emily but her mortal remains as consumption left them. She died December 19, 1848.[10]

2. The Brontë Family

More significant, perhaps, than any personal qualities she might have possessed was Emily's membership of a particular family. The social position of that family was indefinable; the Brontë sisters were the daughters of a clergyman, and that fact alone meant that they could not belong to the working class. But on the other hand, Mr Brontë held the relatively inferior rank of 'perpetual curate' and had himself been born into abject poverty. His parents had occupied a two-roomed cabin in County Down, Northern Ireland, and their son Patrick had worked as a blacksmith, linen-weaver and schoolmaster before obtaining the sizarship at Cambridge which led to his degree and ordination. These humble Irish beginnings were not easily forgotten; his own children were speaking and writing in Irish as well as Yorkshire dialect before they grew up – Charlotte is said to have had a strong Irish accent until well into her teens. Moreover, Mr Brontë was a partisan of the more evangelical tendencies in the church, particularly Methodism, and his disinclination towards the mainstream of Anglicanism would amount to his keeping his distance from the upper class.

Nevertheless, he was socially ambitious. His changing his name from O'Prunty to Brontë while at Cambridge shows this if nothing else does. And if he was socially linked to the working class, he was politically opposed to it. Arriving in Yorkshire when the Luddite campaign was at its fiercest, he immediately enrolled in the service of the Revd Hammond Roberson, the 'clerical dragoon'. What this meant was real action – physical opposition to those who were wrecking the machines. It also meant partial fulfilment of his dream of becoming a soldier, compared to which a priesthood was only second-best (the military profession cut more ice in social terms). Ever afterwards he detested mobs, and would always go to sleep with a loaded and cocked pistol within reach, always rising to fire it from his bedroom window on the following morning. What this shows is not only his need for at least the outward signs of another (and very unpriestly) way of life, but also a state of mind in which he remained almost literally at war with his social inferiors.

Among the other adult influences in the parsonage, Aunt Branwell was chiefly concerned with maintaining the standards of gentility to which she had been accustomed in Penzance. But the fact that the children were using Irish and Yorkshire forms of speech suggests that her impact was much less than that of Tabby, who would have been more of a mother to the children when they were small. Their readiness to identify with Tabby certainly did not fade with their own approach to adulthood; when the elderly housekeeper broke her leg it was the sisters who automatically took upon themselves what their aunt would have regarded as merely servant's work. Charlotte could write at the age of twenty-three: 'Human feelings are queer things; I am much happier black-leading the stoves, making the beds, and sweeping the floors at home than I should be living like a fine lady anywhere else.'[11] Despite the aspirations of their father and aunt, the family remained poor; Emily was frequently unable to afford the postage on letters.

Such an indefinite social position might have been resolved if the Brontës had all been men, with proportionally higher chances of making their own way in the world; the fact that they were (three of them) women placed them at an even greater disadvantage in early Victorian England. And the fact that the only man among them, Branwell, was a complete failure at taking his place in society, suggests that the mental climate in which they were brought up was totally unsuited to the demands of the real world outside the parsonage.

It is easy to see how the Brontës might become psychologically isolated. Even at Haworth they were outsiders; neither their father nor their aunt was a local person (far from it) and indeed their father's appointment as clergyman there was resisted by the parish council, probably on account of his reactionary politics. Within the family there was a further, quite sharp, division between children and adults. Mr Brontë was autocratic in manner towards the girls although indulgent towards Branwell, and took all his meals alone, which must have been estranging. Aunt Branwell undoubtedly meant well, but her replacing their mother seems to have united the children against her rather than endeared her to them. When the imaginary worlds were dreamed of, the children's creative talents were so powerful that it was almost inevitable that fantasy should start to loom larger than reality. Just how extreme their investment in fantasy was, may be judged from the fact that Tabby seriously wondered on occasion whether they were not actually mad:

Leyland recalled a further incident, which he received at first hand from Tabby's nephew, the village carpenter, William Wood, when Tabby was so much alarmed by them that she fled to his cottage out of breath, and cried: 'Willum! Ya mun gooa up to Mr. Bontë's, for aw'm sure yon childer's all goan mad, and aw darn't stop i' the house ony longer wi'en, an'aw'll stay till woll ya come back.' The children were understandably gratified by the success of their acting, and greeted

William Wood when he arrived at the parsonage 'with a great crack o' laughin'' at Tabby's expense.[12]

The high spirits were much less frequent than the deadly earnestness with which Emily, for one, could think, feel, write or speak Gondal almost without intermission. Even in 1845, the year in which she was composing *Wuthering Heights*, she could spend the whole of a journey to York in the company of Anne imagining her sister and herself in a variety of Gondalian situations.

All of this made the gap between the parsonage and the rest of the world disproportionately large, and it has to be said that as often as the Brontës managed to cross that gap, they just as often had to go back the way they had come: Haworth was their only refuge. As educated women who were poorly off, the only social role available to them outside of marriage (Emily never had any offers) was that of governess or teacher. The Brontës' only contacts with the outside world were through education. When they later tried to break this deadlock with the plan of becoming professional writers they could not even begin to make their way without disguising the fact that they were women: 'we had a vague impression that authoresses are liable to be looked on with prejudice; we had noticed how critics sometimes use for their chastisement the weapon of personality, and for their reward, a flattery, which is not true praise'.[13]

The position of governess was such that it could only increase the amount of social insecurity already felt by the Brontës. A governess was a servant of the family for whom she worked, but her education would segregate her from the other servants: she would be the most isolated figure in the house. The position of teacher brought with it the disadvantage of a complete lack of freedom, especially the lack of free time, and this would prove unbearable to women who had already learned the habit of independence. Going away to school, and then to work, was always a mortifying experience, to a greater or lesser extent. When Charlotte and Emily were sent to the Clergy Daughters' School at Cowan Bridge, it did not open any horizons for them: quite the opposite. What was brought home to them was the fact that they were dependent on the charity of others. Despite their youth they must have known obscurely that they were not there for the purpose of cultivating themselves but to serve the purposes of others. They were commencing a process intended to make them useful to their social superiors, who depended on this exploitation of their time, intellect and imagination.

Once the process of education was complete, they were ready to take their place among those whom they might have hoped would treat them, on cultural grounds at least, as equals. But instead of the acceptance which Aunt Branwell's pretensions, their father's ambition and their sense of their own worth might have led them to expect, they only met with social rejection. Their resentment in such a case would have been greater by virtue of the fact that their employers were manifestly their inferiors in respect of taste, learning and abilities. Moreover, they came from a professional family, and they must have been frustrated to learn that this was a useless distinction in the eyes of employers who were often manufacturers. The leisure enjoyed by the families who could offer them work must have rankled with girls who had often had to work with their bare hands at home. Worst of all, they did not even receive better treatment at the hands of employers who were clergymen like their father; nor from those related to clergymen friends of their father. In situations like these, where they were up against small-minded men trying to profit psychologically by the introduction of a few social distinctions where none existed, they must have reacted with exasperation as well as the usual dismay; the only thing that seemed to count was money changing hands.

Terry Eagleton, in his study of the Brontës, argues that the pattern of their careers reflects the general fate of a Romanticism unable to survive the emergence of Victorian industrialism. He describes a process in which the Brontës' authentic mode of existence, the self-fulfilling life of the imagination, is forced to convert itself to use, but in the kind of conditions where the only use that can be made of it destroys its original character.[14] The most compelling illustration of this is the career of Branwell, who should not be seen as the victim of his own peculiar weaknesses but as a typical casualty of the changes in social reality overtaking Britain in the first few decades of the century. Branwell's intellectual amd imaginative training was completely anachronistic; his understanding of the world was Byronic, attuned to the creation of heroic episodes both on and off the page. He was allowed to create an image of himself which could only be pursued in opium or in drink, not in the hard reality which forced him to try and earn a living as a ticket clerk at Sowerby Bridge railway station. If his sisters' education was always conspicuously functional, his was far from being so, and when he was sent away to London with enough money to start an academic training as an artist, his psychology failed to meet the challenge. He drank the money away, and could only face those at home by converting the whole experience into his own terms with the invention of a Byronic adventure in which he had been set upon and robbed.

Given that the only social unit which really worked for the Brontës was comprised of themselves and no others, it is hardly surprising that they made more than one attempt to establish their own school. If they had succeeded in doing so, they would have enjoyed the novel experience of answering to no one but themselves. More than that, they would have reversed the positions in their usual relations with the upper class, who would be sending their daughters to them. It must have been particularly embittering, therefore, when the scheme foundered chiefly through lack of money and social connections.

Clearly, their attachment to each other was more than a source of special strength to the Brontës; it was a necessity. It is all the more remarkable, therefore, that Emily was solitary even within this group. She spoke less, she spent more time alone on the moors and it seems that she genuinely preferred animal to human company. Unlike Charlotte and Anne, she shunned the visits of family friends and acquaintances. But most of all, she was cut off from the others by her irreligiousness. By this, I do not mean to suggest how lonely Emily Brontë must have been, merely to point to the high value she would have to have placed on her sense of community with her brother and sisters. It is worth bearing in mind when considering the meaning of that final phase of non-cooperation with her sisters' publishing ventures, followed by her non-cooperation with the idea of staying alive. It must have seemed as if the family was disintegrating. Charlotte may have excluded Branwell from the *Poems* project; at any rate she was not speaking to him, and her behaviour over the publication of both *Poems* and the novels had turned Emily against her in some degree. Branwell's deterioration had become relentless and only Emily took any proper care of him. When he died, it was already clear that Anne was seriously ill from tuberculosis. One cannot say categorically that Emily wanted to die, nor why she should want to do so, only ponder on the fact that the surest element of continuity in her behaviour, both before her last illness and during it, was the strength of her will.

3. The Brontë Setting

It is not for nothing that the Brontë name has become inseparably linked with that of Haworth. The careers of all three sisters provide telling examples of a Romantic attachment to place, to a particular landscape, not only in their work but in the patterns of their own lives. It is often assumed that the Yorkshire moors stand in a similar relation to the Brontë novels as the lakes and hills of Cumbria do to the poetry of Wordsworth. But that is the trouble: Haworth has become virtually synonymous with a *natural* landscape. Without wishing to play down the evident love of nature shared by the younger members of the Brontë family, it is important to realize how the critics' interest in nature has been strong enough to displace other possible objects of attention. There is no doubt that *Wuthering Heights* is in crucial ways a response to a given environment, but that environment is not composed entirely of stunted trees, rocks, furze and unyielding winds. If one is prepared to extend the range of inquiry, it begins to seem wilful of writers like Winifred Gérin to counterpose the natural environment to the social environment, instead of admitting the presence of both.[15] Because if Haworth was a refuge for the Brontës, it was not in other respects a secluded place. Nothing is more misleading than the image of Emily Brontë as a solitary genius, communing with nature but not with other human beings, totally oblivious to the tide of events surrounding her. Evidently, she was often apart and brooding, but her work alone should tell us that the subject of her brooding was not exclusively nature. As a matter of fact, nature is hardly ever given direct treatment in the novel; most of the scenes are set indoors, including the important ones between Cathy and Heathcliff, who are not presented together in the outdoor environment they are so closely associated with. Associations with nature are built up through the use of figurative language, which has led at least one critic to remark that real nature is actually repressed in the text.[16] The most extensive set of examples of figurative language revolves around the idea of a threshold or barrier between indoors and outdoors, and this gives a fair indication of the extent to which socialization is an issue in the text, not something ignored by it.

Even if Emily Brontë had wanted to ignore the conditions in which others lived and worked she would have had no chance of doing so. We know that her father had wanted to be a man of affairs (when he travelled to Belgium with Emily and Charlotte he registered himself as a *'gérant d'affaires'*) and that he was politically active: as a young Orangeman in Ireland he had helped to put down the rebellion of 1789, and he had afterwards become personally involved in the labour struggles of the West Riding. When at home, he took care to read several newspapers a week, and to pass on their contents to his children. But Emily did not have to rely on the energies and awareness of her father to grasp the realities of social conflict and human suffering; she need only keep her eyes and ears open to the local sights and sounds.

Haworth was not a remote hamlet, but a large village a few miles from Keighley, in one of the most rapidly expanding parts of industrial England. It was close to the centre of the woollen industry, with several worsted mills of its own. The population of the West Riding grew by 73 per cent between 1801 and 1831; that of Keighley went from 3,971 to 5,835 between 1811 and 1831. Against these figures, one should set the harrowing fact that between 1838 and 1849 – the decade when Emily wrote *Wuthering Heights* – 41·6 per cent of the population of Haworth itself died before reaching the age of six.

The West Riding was traditionally the most radical part of England. In fact, the English Civil War began there. The character of the local farmers was described by Thoresby, the Leeds Presbyterian topographer, who identified a 'race of inferior yeomanry' in which could be found 'a spirit of equality and republican independence ... acknowledging no superiors and practising no civilities; a sour and sturdy humour, defiance in every voice and fierceness in every countenance'. Such intractability was not likely to alter much with the growth of prosperity: 'In rank somewhat above there is wealth perpetually increasing but without tendency to civilization, so that a man whose estate would enable him to keep a coach will drive his own cart and is not to be distinguished in gait or dialect from a labourer.'[17] This description of typical attitudes and conduct makes the appearance and behaviour of several characters in *Wuthering Heights* seem much less perverse than it did to the genteel readers of the first few editions of the book.

When the Brontës were still children, a huge proportion of the local population was suffering from the loss of its livelihood, as hand labour was being rapidly replaced by mechanization. Whole families, who had worked for next-to-nothing combing wool in their wretched hill cottages, began to drift down into the villages and towns, often in a starving condition. Women and even children were being forced to scrape a bare living in the new factories. Richard Oastler sent a number of letters about child labour in the worsted mills to the *Leeds Mercury*, one of the papers which was read at the Haworth parsonage. Given the native independence of the textile workers, it is hardly surprising that their sense of grievance and frustration should have modulated into violent protest as their situation steadily worsened. There were riots at Harts-head in 1812 when Mr Brontë was minister there, and machine-breaking continued for many years after the sisters had been born. By the time they were adolescents, Haworth was in the thick of agitation for the Parliamentary Reform Bill:

The district was then swept by riots against the new workhouse law. Their adult years saw periodical storms and riot, for the Ten Hours' Bill and the Factory Acts, or against the Corn Laws and the high price of bread, as well as around the 'Plug' strikes and the three waves of Chartism.[18]

Emily's period of residence at Law Hill above Halifax coincided with the Poor Law riots in that town, and only a few miles away on Hartshead Moor there occurred one of the largest Chartist torchlight rallies. In the Haworth Parsonage Museum today there can be seen a Proclamation of 1838, pronouncing the illegality of all such assemblies. A Parliamentary inquiry revealed the conditions of women working in the mines at Bir-kenshaw (they had to drag the trolleys of coal by chains between their legs), which was only two miles away from Ellen Nussey's home at Gomershall, where Charlotte was, of course, a welcome visitor. By the time the two sisters were ready to leave for Brussels, in 1841, the situation was such that the major-general in command of the Northern Division, Sir Charles Napier, was able to report in a letter: 'Every element of a ferocious civil war is boiling in this district.'

Emily nowhere offers a direct account of these incidents, but the same tones of division and conflict are present throughout her novel. Charlotte does explore some of the major issues in her novel *Shirley*, begun while Emily was still alive. But both sisters were fully aware of the nature of what was happening long before they reached adulthood. As children, they were constructing their imaginary worlds along lines which show, unmistakably, the impact of local events:

Unequivocal symptoms of dissatisfaction began to appear at the same time among the lower orders in Verdopolis. The workmen at the principal mills and furnaces struck for an advance of wages, and, the masters refusing to comply with their exorbitant demands, they all turned out simultaneously. Shortly after, Colonel Grenville, one of the great millowners, was shot. His assassins, being quickly discovered and delivered up to justice, were interrogated by torture, but they remained inflexible, not a single satisfactory answer being elicited from them. The police were now doubled. Bands of soldiers were stationed in the more suspicious

19

parts of the city, and orders were issued that no citizen should walk abroad unarmed.[19]

This is in Charlotte's hand, and it should be recalled that Emily's attachment to the local scene proved to be much stronger than her sister's. Making all due allowances for Charlotte's youth, her reporting of unrest in Glasstown does not find her uneasy in the question of where her loyalty is due. It must have been harder for Emily, because her father's hostility to the strikers was motivated at least partly by the demands of his spiritual allegiance to Methodism, which she was completely out of sympathy with.

The President of the Methodist Conference, throughout the greater part of Patrick Brontë's ministry, was the Revd Jabez Bunting. When Mr Brontë first arrived in the West Riding, he was even more directly under the influence of Bunting while the latter was superintendent minister of the Halifax circuit. Bunting's treatment of the Luddites was merciless. He damned them with 'bell, book and candle', and refused to perform the burial rites over the body of any Methodist involved in the riots. When he became President of the Conference he excommunicated all those ministers who had shown themselves sympathetic towards the radical cause. He was such a hated figure that he was forced to employ a bodyguard, with the sneering comment, 'The bullet is not yet cast that will shoot me.'

There were personal connections between the Brontës and Bunting. Patrick only met his wife, Maria Branwell, because she had come to Yorkshire to help in the founding of a training school for Methodist ministers at Woodhouse Grove. This school had been set up at the instigation of Bunting himself, and Maria Branwell was the niece of its first principal. The very name of the then President of the Conference is similar to that of the Revd Jabes Branderham, who figures so largely in Lockwood's first dream in *Wuthering Heights*. When Lockwood complains of his broken night's sleep to Heathcliff, it is with the suspicion that a family connection is partly to blame: '"I'm not going to endure the persecutions of your hospitable ancestors again. Was not the Reverend Jabes Branderham akin to you on the mother's side?"' (p. 69).

The words and actions of Branderham, which appear at once so laughable and so menacing, correspond closely to the authoritarian doctrines and violent reprisals of Bunting and his followers. We are left in no doubt of the innate brutality of Branderham's position, and it seems more than likely that Emily Brontë would have viewed the Revd Bunting with similar disfavour. Her dilemma would arise with a sense of alienation from her own family's spiritual direction, coupled with the knowledge that any radical presence in Haworth would have regarded the parson's daughter with misgiving. The open avowal on her part of either support or compassion for those without work or redress is unthinkable.* What we should note is the depth of her involvement in the texture of local life and her evident relish for the vernacular of the ordinary people, which is reproduced so accurately in *Wuthering Heights*. It means something that Charlotte was embarrassed by this aspect of the novel when she had to prepare the text for a second edition; she tried to disguise the harshness of the speech and to neutralize the vehemence of the local character with which Emily had kept faith. And if it is true that Emily was inclined to give the popular voice a hearing, there are also signs that her fellow feeling was not restricted to those close to home. In the novel, when Mr Earnshaw returns from a trip to Liverpool, he tells a story of having found Heathcliff 'starving, and houseless, and as good as dumb in the streets' (p. 78). When Emily was writing the novel in the autumn of 1845, Branwell had just returned from a journey to Liverpool, bringing reports of the streets being full of starving children, the victims of the Irish Famine. The young Heathcliff spoke in 'some gibberish that nobody could understand' (p. 77) – just like the children of the Famine, who could only speak Erse. Whatever she heard from her brother would have been offset by the knowledge that collections for the victims of the Famine were being made in Haworth church, which Emily seldom attended. Her novel bears witness to a depth of social division that mere charity would be powerless to undo.

---

* Edward Chitham is prepared to speculate that the 'daring and original ideas' attributed to Emily by Charlotte 'seem likely to have been politically radical or even revolutionary'.[20]

4. Wuthering Heights

At the start of the novel, we are offered the spectacle of a huge social gap opening up between Lockwood, the initial narrator, and Heathcliff, the protagonist (Nelly Dean once refers to her story as 'Heathcliff's history'). Lockwood arrives at the Heights to arrange his accommodation at Thrushcross Grange, of which Heathcliff is the owner. Heathcliff does not enter the story as a great lover, but as a 'landlord' whose position depends on the exercise of power over others. Lockwood has banished himself to this remote part of Yorkshire in a fit of fashionable melancholy, and he stupidly imagines that Heathcliff's apparent misanthropy is also not real but assumed. Both socially and geographically, the two men come from completely different worlds, but it takes a long time for Lockwood to realize what is soon evident to the reader, that his genteel city mentality is completely unable to deal with the world of the Heights; his civilized conciliations are up against something ferociously hostile, and he makes one clumsy error after another.

The first meeting between the two men takes place across a significant barrier, the gate on which Heathcliff leans, and thereafter every kind of distance intervenes, although Lockwood is unable to perceive it. He describes himself as being 'exaggeratedly reserved' (at the same time he says that Heathcliff is more so) and yet from the start he shows every sign of being thoroughly sociable and anxious to remain that way. His first words to Heathcliff are formal – if slightly mechanical – and render all due politeness; when they are met with rudeness he reacts partly by being amused and partly by trying to amuse. His language is conspicuously cultivated, to a degree which may strike the reader as absurd, given its application in a rustic context (he dubs the interior of this forbidding farmhouse a 'penetralium'). In a fairly obvious way, he is being presented as the opposite of Heathcliff; their very names seem designed to contrast with each other: *Lockwood* and *Heathcliff* – the inside and outside of the locked door of civilization. The steady reversal of Lockwood's expectations is clearly designed to reveal his own inadequacies. And in one sense, he is even more cut off from other human beings than Heathcliff himself; he is going to have to interpret a tale of extraordinary passion, and yet the knowledge of passion is something that he has retreated from, as he reveals when explaining the reason for his temporary absence from polite society:

While enjoying a month of fine weather at the sea-coast, I was thrown into the company of a most fascinating creature, a real goddess, in my eyes, as long as she took no notice of me. I 'never told my love' vocally; still, if looks have language, the merest idiot might have guessed I was over head and ears; she understood me, at last, and looked a return – the sweetest of all imaginable looks – and what did I do? I confess it with shame – shrunk icily into myself, like a snail, at every glance retired colder and farther; till, finally, the poor innocent was led to doubt her own senses, and overwhelmed with confusion at her supposed mistake, persuaded her mamma to decamp. (p. 48)

This is the closest that Lockwood gets to involvement with a member of the opposite sex, and yet the language of real feeling is completely absent; instead, we get a winsome compound of conventional phrasing and clichés ('a most fascinating creature', 'a real goddess', etc.). The actual word 'love' can only appear within inverted commas, as if the feeling itself were too naked and uncivilized. And the urgency of Lockwood's recoil from passion is only equalled by the dishonesty of his conduct towards the girl whose interest he has aroused. It is a far cry from the violent directness that Heathcliff is to show in his passion for Cathy, and yet if the two seem furthest apart in respect of their dealings with women, it is precisely in the context of their emotional lives that there exist hidden links between the two men. When Lockwood says that 'Mr Heathcliff may have entirely dissimilar reasons for keeping his hand out of the way, when he meets a would be acquaintance, to those which actuate me' (p. 47) he is partly right, and partly wrong; very roughly speaking, both men have been disappointed in love. The point is that Heathcliff and Lockwood do not stand in a relation of complete opposites so much as in a parodic relationship with each other. Those feelings which are empowered and even let loose by Heathcliff's nature are suppressed and distorted by Lockwood's; yet the pressure of such feelings *is* felt by Lockwood and will be gradually expressed by him, despite the constraint and unnaturalness of the civilized behaviour he is concerned to represent.

Heathcliff is already so implacable and inexorable that to any reader more attentive than Lockwood it seems as if each detail of the Heights is in some way expressive of its master's aggression. The fabric and layout of the building is described in terms of attack and defence: 'corners' are 'defended', while 'the kitchen is forced to retreat'. Just as Heathcliff is obscurely a source of danger so the farmhouse itself is imbued with a sense of mystery, of something hidden: filled with shadows and recesses which do not yield up their meaning. When the dogs have 'issued from hidden dens' to attack the newcomer, it is as if to compensate for the clamped-down natural violence that Heathcliff must hold in check; he contents himself by growling 'in unison' with the dogs. When Lockwood compares this experience to a confrontation with 'the herd of possessed swine' he is lending support to the idea of the hidden power of instinct, as well as preparing for the notion that the Heights may be haunted by evil spirits.

After the canine onslaught, Heathcliff shows the first signs of re-laxation – he is evidently gratified by the display of aggression – and it is interesting that his chief means of reaching a compromise with Lockwood is the adaptation of his language: he 'relaxed, a little, in the laconic style of chipping off his pronouns, and auxiliary verbs' (p. 50). Brontë is being very specific: Heathcliff's is a rather unwilling com-promise, but it alerts us to the importance of language as offering a key to the ratio of social unity and division in a novel whose several nar-rators achieve varying degrees of success in finding the right language to cope with and do justice to the experience confronting them.

Lockwood retires from his first visit to the Heights with his desire for rural seclusion utterly quenched. At the Grange, we see him annoyed at not being able to keep 'civilized' hours, and on his second approach to the Heights, the indignation he directs towards its inhabitants amounts to a complete volte-face from his assumed misanthropy of the day before: '"Wretched inmates!" I ejaculated, mentally, "you deserve perpetual isolation from your species for your churlish inhospitality"' (p. 51). The second time round, he demonstrates that he has learned nothing; when he meets the other members of the household, this only results in his compounding the number of his mistakes. The most distasteful of his blunders arise because he is observing the code of conduct of his class; his reaction towards others depends entirely on his consciousness of their rank, which means that because there is an 'absence of clear proofs' of Hareton's condition, he is blind to the latter's basic decency and rudimentary considerateness. His snobbery becomes unacceptable when he responds to Hareton's dignity with scorn and amusement. He even goes as far as to think of Hareton as 'repulsive', although he has received more courtesy from him than from any other member of the household. His frequently sarcastic thoughts ('I began to feel unmistakably out of place in that pleasant family circle') reveal the insincerity of what he actually says and does, and make an unpleasant contrast with Hareton's candid straightforwardness.

About the younger Catherine he is grotesquely inaccurate: he somehow manages to see in her the sort of qualities that had attracted him in the young lady at the seacoast. Where the reader can perceive all the symptoms of misery and vexation, Lockwood notices chiefly a superficial agreeableness: 'an admirable form, and the most exquisite little face that I have ever had the pleasure of beholding' (p. 53). Lockwood is a poor interpreter of humanity because the range of his perceptions is limited by the narrowness and artificiality of his language. His incredible view of the younger Catherine is due to the fact that his language equips him to see attractive young women as 'beneficent fairies' and as nothing else. When he falls to musing on the possibility of breaking her heart – in the sense in which he had played at flirting with the young lady at the seacoast – his arrogance and self-conceit know no bounds: 'she has thrown herself away upon that boor [Hareton], from sheer ignorance that better individuals existed! A sad pity – I must beware how I cause her to regret her choice' (p. 55).

These misconceptions arise in concert with a whole succession of bad guesses on Lockwood's part: first of all, he expects politeness from the lady of the house, and doesn't get it; then, he refers her to a cushion full of cats – which turns out to be a heap of dead rabbits; he assumes that the younger Catherine is the wife of Heathcliff, and does no better when he recasts her in the role of Hareton's wife; he attributes the paternity of Hareton to Heathcliff, and finally reaches the pitch of absurdity by assuming that Joseph's insult against someone's mother's reputation is meant to refer to himself.

Lockwood is made to appear at his most obtuse when misconstruing the ways in which the various members of the household are related to each other. But, really, this is not a difficult set of mistakes to make. It is usual to find close family relationships existing among people who live in the same house, and Lockwood's exploration, on the reader's behalf, of the tortuous indirectness of the relationships at Wuthering Heights is instructive. It suggests that a closely knit family may be the potential model for harmony in a novel where the loose association of characters at the Heights is the condition of a universal antagonism. (My discussion of the ending of the book will consider the likelihood of this.) By the time that Lockwood is ready to turn his back on the Heights, he has provoked a scene in which everyone's voice is raised against everyone else, and we are given the impression that this is a usual state of affairs.

The scene of uproar occasioned by the visitor's attempt to leave reaches a climax with a second attack by the dogs. Their first assault had seemed like the unleashing of violent natural forces, but this time it is stressed that their brute force is needed to protect the rights of property. Heathcliff had threatened as much, in showing his unwillingness to allow

Lockwood the range of the place, and Joseph makes it plain by summoning the dogs to prevent the theft of his lantern. Part of the novel's purpose is to show how natural instincts can become perverted by the demands of culture. Lockwood, therefore, finds himself at the receiving end of the kind of treatment from which he would normally benefit in his social position. Moreover, the head-on confrontations he is experiencing at the Heights make him impatient of the much more devious routes through which culture usually exercises its rights, and he begins to react in a way which makes his culture seem only skin-deep. For a start, he shows himself capable of as much aggression as his opponents. When he had first been attacked by the bitch pointer, he had flung her back, interposed a table between them, and slashed at the other dogs with a poker. On suspecting that Joseph has insulted him, he very nearly, in his own words, kicks the aged rascal out of the door. And when Heathcliff prevents Hareton from guiding him through the snow, Lockwood seizes the lantern that Joseph has been using and stamps off in a fury. The dogs overpower him, but his subsequent trembling is not out of fear but out of wrath; he is floored, but he proceeds to hurl insults and threats at those who have offended him. Finally, his copious nosebleed is not the result of a physical knock but of 'agitation', which suggests the predominance of nervous impulse over civilized veneer. While the original readers of the novel would have been reassured by the presence of Lockwood in the first few pages, since they would have been closer to him in class than to the inhabitants of the Heights, his initial role of providing an induction to something that would be very foreign to the reader's experience undergoes a transformation once it is seen that the points of difference between Lockwood and Heathcliff do not greatly outweigh the points of similarity.

The continual assertion and contradiction of a barrier between what is 'civilized' and what is 'uncivilized' is maintained throughout the episode of Lockwood's dreams. Just as our first encounter with Heathcliff as landlord rather than lover is significant, so it is important to recognize the meaning of our first encounter with Cathy. We meet her at the very first in *writing*:

It was a Testament, in lean type, and smelling dreadfully musty: a fly-leaf bore the inscription – 'Catherine Earnshaw, her book', and a date some quarter of a century back.

I shut, and took up another, and another, till I had examined all. Catherine's library was select; and its state of dilapidation proved it to have been well used, though not altogether for a legitimate purpose; scarcely one chapter had escaped a pen and ink commentary – at least, the appearance of one – covering every morsel of blank that the printer had left. (p. 62)

Cathy first enters the story through the margins of a 'legitimate' text, which allows the prospect of her being a socially marginalized figure herself. Will her role in the events to be narrated prove to be 'unlawful' in some sense? Will her behaviour strike us as being 'beyond the pale' of what is normally acceptable in either word or deed? As Lockwood reads further in the account inscribed by Cathy in a spirit of rivalry with the 'legitimate' text, he discovers an open expression of her hatred for 'a good book', by which she refers to Joseph's volumes of instruction in orthodox morality. This is plain evidence of a disinclination for acquiring the knowledge of what is according to rule or custom. It is interesting that when Lockwood is subsequently addressed by what is supposed to be the ghost of Cathy, she describes herself as having been a *waif* for twenty years. We tend now to understand by this word 'a neglected child', but in old legal terminology it meant 'a female outlaw'.

Between his discovery of Cathy's diary and his encounter with her apparition, Lockwood has the dream in which he must struggle with Jabes Branderham. In the dream, he is travelling with Joseph in the direction of the chapel where Branderham will preach. Joseph advises him that he will not be able to enter the house without a heavy-headed cudgel; he calls such a cudgel a 'pilgrim's staff' and the discrepancy reminds us of the extent to which orthodoxy may rely on a hidden brute strength. As in waking life, Lockwood misinterprets the words of Joseph, and is about to ridicule the idea that he needs a weapon to enter his own home. The dream commences, then, with a measure of uncertainty about the nature of the relationship between property and violence. Inside the chapel, Branderham delivers a sermon divided into four hundred and ninety parts, 'each fully equal to an ordinary address from the pulpit and each discussing a separate sin!' (p. 65); we can take this as a fairly obvious comment on the tyrannizing scope of conventional morality. When Lockwood grows fatigued, he interrupts this mammoth sermon and is punished. We need not take his defeat as a victory for orthodoxy, merely note that Lockwood's unconscious has searched for and found in Branderham a suitable agency of punishment: i.e. at an unconscious level, Lockwood realizes that he ought to be punished. Branderham denounces him for something *worse than* having gapingly contorted his visage; he performed this action when he grimaced at the dogs, thus provoking their assault, but he also did it when making eyes at the girl at the seaside. His sin, therefore, is the betrayal of genuine feeling. The drubbing he receives has a comic element in it which helps to puncture his self-righteousness, but the reason for his being punished brings seriously into question his substitution of conventional standards of behaviour for a genuine responsiveness to others.

The first dream is fairly easy to recover from, but the second dream shakes Lockwood to the core. It shows him, with a terrifying immediacy, the power of the irrational to overcome resistance. The fact that it is Lockwood who has this dream, rather than one of the other characters, is significant because he is the least likely person to dream it. He has done more than anyone else to shut out of his life the world of instincts and natural forces (and there is an implication of this in his name). This circumstance alone suggests the very real existence of such forces 'deep down' in human nature. Coming after his aggressiveness and his nosebleeds, his trial of strength with the apparition shows how the least civilized part of man can be found even in him.

On the other hand, there are indications that this is not a dream at all, but the visitation of a ghost, or something like it. We pass from an apparent dream to a wide-awake state without being able to detect the moment of transition from the one to the other. The physical effects of the experience are more real than imaginary, and, most curious of all, the 'waif' proclaims herself to be Catherine Linton rather than Catherine Earnshaw: 'why did I think of *Linton*?' says Lockwood, 'I had read *Earnshaw* twenty times for Linton.' We will not have to read very much further before hindsight will allow the 'creature' an even greater measure of autonomy from Lockwood's imagination. But in any case, the most horrific aspect of the scene is not the awfulness of the supernatural but the shock of Lockwood's reaction to it:

As it spoke, I discerned, obscurely, a child's face looking through the window – terror made me cruel; and, finding it useless to attempt shaking the creature off, I pulled its wrist on to the broken pane, and rubbed it to and fro till the blood ran down and soaked the bedclothes: still it wailed, 'Let me in!' and maintained its tenacious gripe, almost maddening me with fear.

'How can I!' I said at length. 'Let *me* go, if you want me to let you in!'

The fingers relaxed, I snatched mine through the hole, hurriedly piled the books up in a pyramid against it, and stopped my ears to exclude the lamentable prayer. (p. 67)

If it is not a dream, what are we to make of Lockwood's performing this act of savagery *after* he has recognized that he is dealing with a child? Either way, it means that the barrier separating Lockwood and civilization from the world of the moors and what they stand for is as thin and brittle as a pane of glass. When the irrational bursts in upon conscious life and makes its presence felt, the violence exerted by 'culture' against 'nature' in order to redress the balance can be absolutely ferocious; we are offered the spectacle of a so-called civilized gentleman deliberately forcing a child's arm down on to broken glass. If the episode corresponds to the disclosure of a secret desire which is then immediately driven back, there is no reason why we should not attend to the sexual overtones of a ruptured barrier and the blood of a pubescent child soaking the bedclothes. Lurid as this may seem, it fits in with what we know of Lockwood's repressed and voyeuristic sexuality from his own account of his seaside adventure. And when Heathcliff brings Lockwood to account for the events of the night, he is scandalized by the information that Lockwood has made himself doze off ' "in spelling over the name scratched on that window-ledge. A monotonous occupation, calculated to set me asleep, like counting, or –"' (p. 69). The insinuation that Lockwood's thoughts had drifted from the rather empty satisfaction of a girl's name to something literally unmentionable is not lost upon Heathcliff, who loses his temper at this point.[21] The shedding of the child's blood uncovers a disturbing possibility, but in the very same moment it is made known, it is covered up again; from trying to let go of the child's arm, Lockwood suddenly tightens his grip upon it, thus repeating the action of the first dream in which he had tried to grab hold of Joseph's club – the so-called 'pilgrim's staff' of brutal, but legitimate, subjugation. Lockwood then manages to break contact with the child through trickery; and he tries to make certain of shutting out this creature derived from the margins of a 'legitimate' text by replacing the original barrier with a pyramid of *books*. One critic has ingeniously taken note of the fact that Cathy's diary occupies the margins of an 'injured tome' and, exploiting the punning potential of the word, has observed that 'The *pyramid* of books closes the space opened by the injured *tome*'. In other words, Lockwood has employed the sheer weight of legitimacy (which is built to last) in consigning Cathy to the *tomb*.[22] He has been faced with the irruption of lawless forces into his well-ordered life, and he has inwardly mustered all the resources of 'culture' in trying to negate those forces, in trying to consign them to non-existence. It seems that Cathy is forced to exist in another world because the attitude which Lockwood represents will not allow her a place in this one. In 1845, when Emily Brontë was writing this novel, what lay beyond the control of culture was not known as the unconscious; it had to appear in the guises of crime, madness, nature and death. Cathy and Heathcliff have their very beings in the context of all of these. For the moment, it is enough to join this observation with another one, namely that Lockwood dreams his dream, or has his vision, in a coffin-like bed described as a 'large oak case.' It had in fact been Cathy's own bed, and its sliding panel makes it resemble her coffin, one of whose sides Heathcliff bribes the sexton to make loose. Eventually, it becomes Heathcliff's coffin, as he dies in it, leaving open the window which communicates with the world of the moors, the setting of his inordinate passion. In this, Lockwood is once again straying in the direction of a community of impulse and action with Heathcliff; his barbaric treatment of the figure of the waif will be echoed in the account of Heathcliff's skirmish with Hindley, when the two grapple over a window-sill, and Heathcliff slits the flesh of Hindley's wrist before knocking down the window-post which prevents his gaining access to the house. The point being constantly made by these opening chapters hinges on the similarities and differences between the two men. At first, Lockwood is keen to observe the parallels between Heathcliff and himself, but they are the kind of parallels which the reader swiftly recognizes as groundless; once the situation develops, a different set of correspondences begins to emerge which the reader recognizes as authentic but which strikes panic into Lockwood, who does everything he can to revoke his original claims.

When the terrors of the night have abated for Lockwood, he makes haste to pull himself together, and to put up his usual social defences. He interprets Heathcliff's 'agitation' as 'cowardice', which shows a remarkable lack of imagination in one who has so recently learned of the connection between Cathy and Heathcliff. Heathcliff understandably wants information, and he wants it fast, but Lockwood automatically starts to employ insincerity and deceit in editing his version of events; he even presumes to stand on his dignity when Heathcliff loses patience with his prevarications.

Heathcliff is in a state of nervous collapse, and it is a matter for wonder that after twenty years he can still be so affected by what is, after all, a secondhand experience of Cathy. But for Lockwood, such passion is simply embarrassing, and he has to resort to the gentility of performing his 'toilette' in order to cover his embarrassment. He makes himself scarce as soon as he can, but not before thinking out a philosophical-sounding pretext for his lack of fellow-feeling: 'A sensible man ought to find sufficient company in himself' (p. 70). Even at his most sympathetic, Lockwood still designates the passion of Heathcliff as a form of 'raving' or 'folly'.

By the time he has reached the more civilized environment of Thrushcross Grange, he has fully regained his composure, mentally if not physically. In this context, he knows exactly where he stands and exactly what is due to him; his language resumes its affectations, revealing the inherent corruptness in his dealings with others. When Nelly and the other servants rush to greet him, he calls them 'my human fixture and her satellites' (p. 73) – a typical phrase: calculated to amuse, but demeaning at the same time. Once he has recovered to the extent of wanting to satisfy his curiosity about Heathcliff, he has to employ subterfuge to obtain the desired information. It isn't an accident that he uses a military metaphor to convey the mood in which he approaches the idea of social intercourse with an inferior; coming down to Nelly Dean's level is like being 'finally compelled to strike my colours' (p. 74), as if condescending to speak to a servant involved an unwilling suspension of violence.

It is often assumed that violence is typically found at Wuthering Heights, but Lockwood's sophisticated vocabulary of antagonism helps us to realize that violence may be equally at home in the cultivated milieu of Thrushcross Grange.

5. Thrushcross Grange

When Lockwood is resident at Thrushcross Grange, the house is undergoing a lapse in its fortunes; the traditional owners are not there, having either died out or been debarred from their inheritance. We do not see it functioning as the most important place, socially, in the district, except in memory or, at the end of the book, in prospect. Our first introduction to it in this state is through Heathcliff's account (relayed by Nelly) of his and Cathy's reconnoitring it as children. At this point, Wuthering Heights is under the regime of Hindley, who has recently returned there in mysterious possession of 'culture', a fact which is indicated by his speaking and dressing 'quite differently'. Having learned the meaning of culture, he proceeds to impose unnatural social divisions upon the household, obliging Joseph and Nelly to quarter themselves in the back-kitchen so as to leave the main rooms for his personal use. Heathcliff he intends to force apart from Cathy, and 'swears he will reduce him to his right place' (p. 64). From this time on, the children become less and less socialized, and their natural alliance in opposition to their elders starts to become linked with their attachment to the moors – the only place they can be themselves. On one particularly dreary Sunday, when the children are forced to exchange the warmth of the sitting-room for the cold of the back-kitchen, they decide to make the best of their situation, and go for a ramble on the moors: 'and getting a glimpse of the Grange lights, we thought we would just go and see whether the Lintons passed their Sunday evenings standing shivering in corners' (p. 88). Just as the reader is introduced to Wuthering Heights through the eyes of an outsider, Lockwood, so the Grange is first seen by outsiders, the disadvantaged children who catch a glimpse of its alien life-style through the barrier of a window:

We crept through a broken hedge, groped our way up the path, and planted ourselves on a flower-pot under the drawing-room window. The light came from thence; they had not put up the shutters, and the curtains were only half closed. Both of us were able to look in by standing on the basement, and clinging to the ledge, and we saw – ah! it was beautiful – a splendid place carpeted with crimson, and crimson-covered chairs and tables, and a pure white ceiling bordered by gold, a shower of glass-drops hanging in silver chains from the centre, and shimmering with little soft tapers. Old Mr and Mrs Linton were not there. Edgar and his sister had it entirely to themselves; shouldn't they have been happy? We should have thought ourselves in heaven! And now, guess what your good children were doing? Isabella – I believe she is eleven, a year younger than Cathy – lay screaming at the farther end of the room, shrieking as if witches were running red-hot needles into her. Edgar stood on the hearth weeping silently, and in the middle of the table sat a little dog shaking its paw and yelping, which, from their mutual accusations, we understood they had nearly pulled in two between them. (p. 89)

We first encounter Edgar and Isabella, the children of the Grange, engaged in an argument over property. They have almost pulled the small dog apart, and from this moment there begins a process which is almost literally to pull Cathy apart. Her fascination with the splendour of the place is registered by Heathcliff when he includes her in his remark 'We should have thought ourselves in heaven!' His own psychological distance from the nature of what lies in front of him is made plain by his subsequently wondering, 'When would you catch me wishing to have what Catherine wanted?' The two intruders cannot refrain from laughing at the spoiled Edgar and Isabella, who promptly raise the alarm, galvanizing the household into action. The Lintons immediately assume that there is a threat to their property, and they counter that threat with guns, dogs, and even a promise of the gallows. Old Mr Linton identifies himself as the local magistrate, stressing his power as a law-maker; this focuses attention on the link between conventional morality and the division of property. As with Lockwood at the Heights, the façade of respectability is genuinely a façade, hiding a potential for brutality equal to anything the 'uncivilized' world can manage. Once again, there is a sexual overtone in the wound received by the pubescent Cathy, a wound which makes Mrs Linton afraid that 'she may be lamed for life' (p. 91). Feminist critics have made a contrast between the female bitch pointer which guards the Heights, and the masculine bulldog which, with its 'huge purple tongue hanging half a foot out of his mouth, and his pendant lips streaming with bloody slaver' (p. 90), is taken as a symbolic representative of Thrushcross Grange.[23] Apart from the sexual nuance, the idea that Cathy may be lamed for life is borne out by the transformation of her idea of herself that Thrushcross Grange effects from this moment onwards. Heathcliff's defiance is in vain when he says that 'if Catherine had wished to return, I intended shattering their great glass panes to a million of fragments, unless they let her out' (p. 91); from now on, Cathy, without fully realizing it, does *not* wish to return – she prefers to stay on the other side of the window. Of course, her fate is not sealed by her own desire alone but by the attitude of the Lintons, who fairly rapidly distinguish between her and Heathcliff. Like Lockwood, they are guided by the consciousness of rank: although the children have done, or have omitted to do, the same deed, Heathcliff is discriminated against. Cathy is treated as the daughter of a landowner, Heathcliff as a 'thief' and a 'villain'. What helps the Lintons to make this discrimination is Heathcliff's use of language. By his own admission, he utters 'curses enough to annihilate any fiend in christendom', and follows this up by 'grumbling execrations and vengeance' (p. 90); he is so 'foul-mouthed' that Mrs Linton finds him 'quite unfit for a decent house! Did you notice his language, Linton? I'm shocked that my children should have heard it' (p. 91). Such a remark might pass in the drawing-room, but it is the Lintons who have just committed an act of violence, not Heathcliff. Graham Holderness is surely right when he comments, 'the harsh and violent directness of [Heathcliff's] speech seems to express the truth of the situation, while the language of the Lintons mystifies *their* violence by attributing it to the outsider.'[24]

Heathcliff is forced to leave Cathy at Thrushcross Grange and she remains there for five weeks, during which time the process of turning her into a young lady becomes irreversible. When she eventually returns to the Heights she is greeted with Isabella's pronouncement that 'you look like a lady now' (p. 93). But Nelly approves of the change, and responds to the new denominations of 'Ellen' and 'Miss Catherine', in place of 'Nelly' and 'Cathy'. Cathy offers her a kiss, but with a measure of aloofness, since Nelly is covered with flour from preparing a Christmas cake. The new clothes which Cathy would prefer to keep clean are totally impractical in a farmhouse, where it is impossible to ignore the absolute necessity of manual work. Cathy's own hands are now enveloped in gloves which, when removed, display 'fingers wonderfully whitened with doing nothing, and staying indoors' (p. 94). The unreality of this circumstance is unwittingly hinted at in the wording of Nelly's admiration of this 'bright, graceful damsel' who has entered the house.

Hindley, meanwhile, does everything he can to widen the gap that has opened up between Cathy and Heathcliff, emphasizing the latter's demotion to the level of 'the other servants', and using every occasion to humiliate him: '"Shake hands, Heathcliff" said Mr Earnshaw, conde-scendingly: "once in a way, that is permitted."' (p. 94). But the tragedy of Cathy and Heathcliff is not that Cathy has changed out of all recognition, but that her transformation is incomplete: she still feels the tug of old allegiances as much as the desire to set her sights on something new. This is first made clear in her reaction to the dogs which bound up to welcome her; on the one hand, 'her eyes sparkled joyfully', while on the other, 'she dare hardly touch them' (p. 93). This equivocalness is much

more apparent in the crucial test of her reunion with Heathcliff. At first
sight of him, she 'flew to embrace him' (p. 94), showing the presence of
the old Cathy in verbs of vigorous action and human contact. But after
the first flush of her excitement has faded, she thinks twice of this
unlady-like action and tries to save face by laughing at Heathcliff's
appearance. This is a shade too heartless, as she soon acknowledges by
trying to rationalize her being amused: 'It was only that you looked odd'
(p. 96). She is wholly unable to find the right tone with which to address
her old friend in his new status:

She gazed concernedly at the dusky fingers she held in her own, and also at her
dress, which she feared had gained no embellishment from its contact with his.
   'You needn't have touched me!', he answered, following her eye and snatching
away her hand. 'I shall be as dirty as I please, and I like to be dirty, and I will be
dirty.'
   With that he dashed head foremost out of the room, amid the merriment of the
master and mistress; and to the serious disturbance of Catherine, who could not
comprehend how her remarks should have produced such an exhibition of bad
temper. (p. 95)

Heathcliff is quite naturally incensed at Cathy's behaviour; he does not
look half as 'odd' as she does in her finery. It was only five weeks before
that the two of them had been content to share the same cloak for their
scamper over the moors. His over-reaction – insisting on the virtue of
being dirty – is perfectly understandable if we remember the importance
of the outdoors in his relationship with Cathy. And now she is falling in
with all of Hindley's designs. It is hardly surprising that he dashes from
the room, with Hindley's laughter ringing in his ears, in despair at the
realization that she simply does not know what she is doing.
   Cathy spends the rest of the evening preparing for the visit of the
young Lintons on the following day; she only once finds the time to seek
out her former playmate, and when she does not find him in the kitchen,
she evidently thinks it either unnecessary or improper for her to look
further. Heathcliff goes to bed without his supper, and in the morning
rises early to get out on to the moors which had always been the scene of
his unity with Catherine, and the symbol of their division from all others.
To revisit the scene of their greatest intimacy could only make worse his
present feeling of loneliness, and he returns from his walk chastened and
ready to adjust somewhat to the new state of affairs. As Nelly recalls,
'He hung about me for a while, and having screwed up his courage,
exclaimed abruptly, "Nelly, make me decent, I'm going to be good."' (p.
96). It is important that it is Heathcliff who makes this compromise and

not Cathy; the fact that he makes the first move, the first concession, means that his priorities are more human and less selfish than hers. We should note at this point, as a prelude to our later discussion of Nelly Dean, Nelly's moralizing over Heathcliff's behaviour. She categorizes experience in ways that are not just unhelpful but misleading as well; she commends Heathcliff for having rescinded his pride but, really, pride is Cathy's new affliction and Heathcliff has been suffering rather from humiliation justifiably resented. Whatever her motives or the nature of her influence, Nelly succeeds in preparing Heathcliff for his entrée into polite society. But she has not reckoned with the degree of Hindley's enmity; as soon as Heathcliff presents himself, Hindley casts him into the role of common criminal, just as the Lintons had done: '"send him into the garret till dinner is over. He'll be cramming his fingers in the tarts, and stealing the fruit, if left alone with them a minute"' (p. 98). Heathcliff can see that his efforts are useless, but it only needs Edgar to pass one tactless remark in apparent compliance with Hindley's slander, for Heathcliff to play into the latter's hands and lose control of himself: he flings a tureen of hot apple sauce into Edgar's face. In the uproar that follows, Cathy's reactions are strangely inconsistent: she is angry with Heathcliff, but on the whole she is more sympathetic towards him than towards Edgar, for whom she feels considerable contempt. The terms of her exasperation over the likely consequences show a curious blend of compassion and self-centredness: '"I hate him to be flogged! I can't eat my dinner. Why did you speak to him, Edgar?"' (p. 99). It is true that, once the Lintons have left, and in spite of her new manners and splendour, Cathy is found acting the tomboy once more, climbing in and out of skylights to communicate with Heathcliff. But it soon becomes clear that the chief lesson she learns from the episode is not so much the overriding importance of her affection for Heathcliff as the need for more shrewdness in her dealings with the Lintons.

Nelly's account moves forward one year, by which time Cathy has developed into a much more skilful manager of her own affairs:

Catherine had kept up her acquaintance with the Lintons since her five weeks' residence among them; and as she had no temptation to show her rough side in their company, and had the sense to be ashamed of being rude where she experienced such invariable courtesy, she imposed unwittingly on the old lady and gentleman, by her ingenious cordiality; gained the admiration of Isabella, and the heart and soul of her brother – acquisitions that flattered her from the first, for she was full of ambition – and led her to adopt a double character without exactly intending to deceive any one. (p. 107)

The vocabulary in this description of Cathy's social evolution has some very unattractive overtones of calculation and acquisitiveness. It is not being regardless of Nelly's disclaimer in the final clause to assert that Cathy is deceiving herself far more than she is deceiving anyone else. It is obvious from the start that she loves Heathcliff for himself, and Linton only for what he represents. But it is beyond her present powers of comprehension to see that what presents itself now as the problem of a division between herself and her childhood friend is really the reflection of a profound division within her own self, the insuperable 'doubleness' that Nelly's description spells out. Despite the crucial role of the Lintons and Thrushcross Grange in supplying the incentive for this doubleness, it is only fair to consider the evidence for this trait being inherent in Cathy's nature.

There is one important clue for the reader searching for the psychological roots of Cathy's dilemma. Just before old Mr Earnshaw leaves for his trip to Liverpool he asks his children what gifts they would like to receive on his return. Their responses reveal their most cherished desires and, therefore, something of their own natures. Hindley asks for a violin, an unmistakably 'cultural' object which shows he has pretensions beyond the world of the Heights. But Cathy requests a whip, revealing a desire for power and control at a certain cost to sensitivity. In the event, what they get is Heathcliff, who represents something in simple opposition to Hindley's desires, but who offers a much more complex alternative to Cathy. Her love for Heathcliff never dies out, but equally that childhood itch for superiority proves impossible to deny.

For Heathcliff, the passing of one year has brought a complete loss of the means of education; Hindley has deprived him of books and tuition, so that he has been progressively unsocialized. In fact, the only sense of personal value he has now is defined by his opposition to civility. And he has learned to mistrust Cathy, because she has started being deceitful towards him as well as towards the Lintons. On one occasion, he finds her preparing for a visit from Edgar Linton, when 'she had not reckoned on his taking it into his head to be idle, and had therefore imagined that she would have the whole place to herself' (p. 109). On his asking whether she is expecting someone, she lies outright; and when he points out that she spends much more time with Edgar than with him, she avoids an emotional crisis by adopting the haughty tones of Thrushcross Grange to attack him at his most sensitive point – his lack of 'culture':

'And should I always be sitting with you?' she demanded, growing more irritated. 'What good do I get – what do you talk about? You might be dumb or a baby for anything you say to amuse me, or for anything you do, either!'

'You never told me before that I talked too little, or that you disliked my company, Cathy!' exclaimed Heathcliff, in much agitation.

'It's no company at all, when people know nothing and say nothing,' she muttered. (p. 110)

Thus, Cathy starts to employ 'civilized' criteria much more directly in her dealings with Heathcliff, and to judge him by them. But if her letting him know that she regards him in the light of an amenity is only said in the heat of the moment to get rid of him, her treatment of Nelly suggests a much more deliberate and chronic readiness to abuse others. When Edgar arrives, Cathy naturally wants to see him alone, but there is more than a touch of the girl who wanted to wield a whip in her graceless dismissal of an old family servant. When Nelly objects to leaving the room, Cathy rounds on her: ' "I hate you to be fidgeting in my presence," exclaimed the young lady imperiously' (p. 111). It is almost grotesque, in a place like Wuthering Heights, to hear necessary work described as 'fidgeting' by someone who relies on others to do it for her. When Nelly (under orders from Hindley) persists in her stubbornness, Cathy reverts in a flash to completely uncivilized behaviour, trying to wrench Nelly's arm without Edgar seeing. Nelly displays the 'decided purple witness' of the offence, and gets a slap on the face for her pains. The knowledge that Cathy has started to abuse servants physically (in the way that Hindley has always abused Heathcliff) greatly shocks Edgar, who is unused to such a manifest degree of 'falsehood and violence'. A crisis is reached when the infant Hareton adds his voice to the chorus of protests and is made to pay for it: 'she seized his shoulders, and shook him till the poor child waxed livid' (p. 111). At this point Edgar intervenes, with predictable results: Cathy has at least one blow to spare for him. He retreats in disgust at this barbarism, but at the last moment is unable to tear himself away. There is no denying the extremism of Cathy's behaviour, but Edgar's turning back is explained in terms which cast doubt on the meaning of the whole episode:

The soft thing looked askance through the window – he possessed the power to depart, as much as a cat possesses the power to leave a mouse half killed, or a bird half eaten. (p. 112)

The curious thing is that this simile is wholly inappropriate with reference to the personalities involved – Cathy has been acting like the cat, Edgar like the mouse. And yet the simile puts it the other way round; the only way it can be made to work is with reference to the relevant social positions of the personalities involved. Viewed in such a light, what it says is that the Grange – with Edgar as its agent – represents the lack of real feeling, and that Cathy's meanness and cruelty are the result of confusion, not of policy. The simile is rather a blunt instrument; even when we see its rough point, we cannot excuse Cathy's behaviour because it is supposed not to be her fault. All that we can do is to agree that the ultimate responsibility for it lies less in her own psychology than in the influence of Thrushcross Grange.

The tension which underlies this incident is maintained until Heathcliff's departure from the Heights. The decisive factor in this – his supposition that Cathy has finally rejected him – will be discussed in the following section of this study. In the meantime, we may concentrate on the effect of Heathcliff's departure on those who are left behind. Cathy suffers a complete breakdown; her symptoms are uncontrollable grief, inarticulacy, delirium and fever. Once she is faced with the genuine possibility of separation from Heathcliff she is literally beside herself, and unable to function. Unfortunately, her convalescence takes place at Thrushcross Grange, and from this second stay she returns even haughtier and more aloof than before. The psychological mechanism by which she compensates for the loss of one half of her 'doubleness' by a proportionally greater investment in the other half, should not cause much dismay. Nelly accidentally puts her finger on the latent social violence involved, in her grumbling comment, 'it was nothing less than murder, in her eyes, for any one to presume to stand up and contradict her' (p. 128). At Thrushcross Grange, violence can always be mystified by the language of culture; but Wuthering Heights is not yet secure in the possession of culture, and for a social climber like Hindley, tyrannical behaviour and the loss of a common regard for others are necessary proof of one's elevation over others. Accordingly, 'He was rather *too* indulgent in humouring her caprices . . . she might trample us like slaves for aught he cared!' (p. 128).

One should beware of giving the impression that Cathy is only violent because she has learned how to be violent at Thrushcross Grange. Her nature is an essentially volatile one, as is stressed when Nelly comes to review the aftermath of her marriage to Edgar. They are married within three years of Heathcliff's leaving the Heights, but the apparent harmony in which they live is radically insecure because it relies on the most important part of Cathy's nature remaining hidden: 'for the space of half a year, the gunpowder lay as harmless as sand, because no fire came near to explode it' (p. 131). Here, it is being suggested that Cathy's everyday violence – the fact that she is liable to flare up at any moment – is an index of her readiness to revert to an original state, even at a moment's notice. Once she is transplanted to the context of the Grange, she is both 'imperious' and tyrannical to those around her; but this is only partly because she has been brought up in a situation of open conflict under Hindley's regime, a conflict which has been both sharpened and disguised by the need to fulfil her social ambitions. Her aggressiveness is also partly explained by the fact that living at Thrushcross Grange only satisfies her on one level, while on another level it is constantly grating against her sense of her real self.

The point is underlined a few pages later, when Nelly has to bring the news of Heathcliff's return to the unsuspecting couple. She finds them seated at a window in what she takes to be a state of perfect peace. But in recalling the scene through the window, she mentions not only what is visible but also what is *invisible:* 'Wuthering Heights rose above this silvery vapour – but our old house was invisible – it rather dips down on the other side' (p. 133). The peacefulness of the scene depends on Wuthering Heights being kept out of sight, but it's there all the same. We know that peacefulness is not really in Cathy's nature, which is like gunpowder; just like Wuthering Heights, her real self is only obscured, out of sight for the moment, but none the less always there. The actual reunion of Cathy and Heathcliff is not described; Nelly does not witness it. What she does see is Cathy returning, utterly changed from her state of peacefulness to one of violent activity. She *flies* upstairs, *breathless* and *wild, pants* as she *flings* her arms around Edgar, and *tightens* her embrace to a *squeeze.* To Edgar, such physicality is distasteful, and he responds to this show of affection as if it were a threat to his very being: '"don't strangle me . . . There is no need to be frantic!"' (p. 134). When Heathcliff is brought in to make his peace, Cathy *springs* forward, *seizes* Edgar's 'reluctant fingers' and *crushes* them into Heathcliff's. Edgar fails to reintroduce the social distinction by which Heathcliff is of inferior rank (Cathy sidesteps the attempt by pronouncing herself a member of the lower orders) and has to resort to a strained politeness under cover of which he ignores the existence of Heathcliff's passion. Within a few short hours, Cathy has laid bare the reality behind the 'peacefulness' of her marriage: 'agony', 'bitter misery' and an irreconcilability towards both God and man. The husband whom Nelly had thought the object of devotion is now referred to as 'that creature'.

Edgar's problems are not confined to the disaffection of his wife, since the other woman in his care, his sister, develops an irresistible attraction towards Heathcliff. Nelly says that Edgar is appalled at this simply because of his tender love for his sister, but the other reason she gives sounds more likely if we remember how little tenderness Edgar is to show towards Isabella in her disgrace:

Leaving aside the degradation of an alliance with a nameless man, and the possible fact that his property, in default of heirs male, might pass into such a one's power, he had sense to comprehend Heathcliff's disposition – to know that, though his exterior was altered, his mind was unchangeable, and unchanged. (p. 140)

What Nelly asks us to leave aside is actually Edgar's first consideration. It would be tasteless to admit that property comes before everything else, but there is no ignoring the business-like language with which the subject is introduced. Heathcliff would not present a threat if he were completely unchanged; he is only dangerous precisely *because* he has changed – he has learned to think in the Grange way, as Edgar – despite Nelly's understanding of him – realizes only too well. Once again, we are presented with the idea that culture's advantage over nature is the ability to clothe in a moderate form what would be too extreme if expressed directly. There is a huge contrast between the kinds of language employed by Edgar and Heathcliff, when talking about the same thing. This is Edgar, first, addressing Heathcliff:

Your presence is a moral poison that would contaminate the most virtuous – for that cause, and to prevent worse consequences, I shall deny you, hereafter, admission into this house, and give notice, now, that I require your instant departure. Three minutes' delay will render it involuntary and ignominious. (p. 153)

The syntax and vocabulary here are ponderously Latinate and forensic (it is not for nothing that Edgar is a magistrate, freshly returned from a 'justice-meeting'); it comes almost as a surprise when we realize that what he is actually referring to is physical action, the threat of having Heathcliff thrown out of doors. Contrast this with the bluntness of Heathcliff's response:

'Cathy, this lamb of yours threatens like a bull!' he said. 'It is in danger of splitting its skull against my knuckles. By God, Mr Linton, I'm mortally sorry that you are not worth knocking down!' (p. 153)

Edgar's veiled savagery, and Heathcliff's defiance of it, are virtually a repetition of the scene in which the swearing, cursing young Heathcliff finds himself at the mercy of unforgiving, yet equivocating, gentlefolk.

With the disappearance of Cathy's hope for an existence in which there is a place for both Heathcliff and Edgar, the action enters a phase in which she is slowly but surely torn apart. The competing demands of the two men are so utterly opposed to each other, representative of such entirely different worlds, that she cannot possibly sustain them both, still less fulfil the demands of both. So confused is her sense of her own identity that she begins to be unable to recognize her own reflection in the mirror. The need to be detached from her present situation turns into a full-scale illness, in which she imagines herself to be at Wuthering Heights or on the moors, as if her real self is not to be found in her physical body at the Grange. In her delirium, the seven years that separate her from her childhood simply disappear, and she rediscovers with a pang the strength of her original attachment to Heathcliff, who is once more 'my all in all', while the terrible unnaturalness of life at the Grange is summed up as being 'the wife of a stranger; an exile, and outcast, thenceforth, from what had been my world' (p. 163). To Nelly, this is 'insanity', but the reader can appreciate the sense in which it is a lucid interval in a wrong-headed career. Now Cathy can 'see' what has been concealed; in fact, she claims to be able to see the lighted windows of Wuthering Heights, which is an impossibility. She is finally realizing the true value of what she has lost, but the savage irony of this moment is that while she is committing herself to Heathcliff once more, he is committing his greatest treachery against her by eloping with Isabella.

Cathy is never again shaken from her fixation on the Heights until the moment of her death. Edgar can find no comfort except in the discovery that she is pregnant: 'we cherished the hope that in a little while, Mr Linton's heart would be gladdened, and his lands secured from a stranger's gripe, by the birth of an heir' (p. 172). This time, it is expressed much more peremptorily how matters of property hold equal place with gladness of heart. Edgar makes his priorities clear enough when his tender love for his sister is replaced by the decision that they 'are eternally divided' by her offence to propriety. Isabella's own account of her elopement with Heathcliff is so timed as to offer a comparison with the situation of Cathy; the one woman is grieving over her exchange of the Heights for the Grange, while the other is regretting her exchange of the Grange for the Heights. Isabella's letter detailing her arrival at the Heights recalls the opening of the book and Lockwood's confrontation with something he cannot begin to understand, but on this occasion the violent clash between the world of the Heights and the world of the Grange is even more noticeable. It would seem as if the inhabitants of the two houses spoke entirely different languages; Isabella is simply unable to understand what Hareton is saying: 'He replied in a jargon I did not comprehend' (p. 174), while Joseph is similarly dismayed by Isabella's forms of address:

'Mim! mim! mim! Did iver Christian body hear owt like it? Minching un' munching! Hah can Aw tell whet ye say?' (p. 174)

The uncompromising presence of Joseph's dialect plays an important role in the theme of cultural conflict. Joseph is scandalized by Isabella's aristocratic conceptions, latching on to words like *parlour* and *bedroom* (which he calls 'bed-rume') as terms which hold no meaning for him. Isabella tries desperately to preserve the usual social distinctions, asking misguidedly for a maidservant, and when Hareton appears, she anxiously works out his social standing before deciding whether or not she can shake hands with him. It does not take long for her to start yearning for her real home, Thrushcross Grange, and this is counterpointed by Cathy's longing for Wuthering Heights; they each show the same inability to transplant themselves from the one milieu to the other.

Isabella is the victim of her own misconceptions; she has seen in Heathcliff what she wanted to see – a Byronic hero. But she is not entirely to blame for this because Heathcliff has deliberately exploited her interest in him as a means of gaining revenge on Edgar and the Grange. He is also showing Cathy what he takes to be the meaning of her own marriage to Edgar by offering her the spectacle of a loveless match made purely for the sake of material advantage. His abuse of Isabella makes us view her experience at the Heights in a different light to that of Lockwood's, despite the similarities. Lockwood is a man, and this simple fact means that he can retreat unscathed from any romantic entanglement. (As a matter of fact, this is precisely what he has done.) But the ruling values of his society – the values of Thrushcross Grange – are such that what is possible for him is unavailable to a woman. Isabella has nowhere to go. And that is precisely where she does go; tyrannized by her husband, rejected by her brother, she disappears to give birth somewhere beyond the pale of respectable society. Her social nothingness is parallelled by her exit from the text.*

The constant, uneasy tension between the meaning of Wuthering Heights and the meaning of Thrushcross Grange is brought into simple focus with the death and burial of Cathy. Just after her death, Nelly discovers a locket in which Cathy had always kept a lock of Edgar's hair: 'Heathcliff had opened the trinket and cast out its contents,

---

* Heathcliff's strategy, involving the seizure of the Linton property, depends on the fact that both at the time the novel is set and at the time it was written, wives had no right to their own property or earnings. They continued to be denied this right until 1870 when the Married Women's Property Act was introduced. Moreover, any woman wishing to divorce her husband would have had small hope of doing so before the advent of the Matrimonial Causes Act of 1857. Well before that date, Heathcliff could rely on the knowledge that his wife was legally and economically subservient to him. Isabella could enjoy only the narrow privilege of custody of a child less than seven years old; if her child had been any older, she would have had only limited access to him.

replacing them by a black lock of his own. I twisted the two, and enclosed them together' (p. 205). The two locks of hair symbolize the impossible, rival claims which had become inextricable in Cathy – trying to untangle them had killed her. Heathcliff's action in supplanting Edgar's hair with his own is true to the manner of Cathy's death, but Nelly's amendment of this, while it is typical of her own meddling role in the history of the two houses, is an appropriate comment on the complexity of Cathy's life. Her 'double nature' is even expressed by the siting of her grave, right at the edge of the churchyard 'where the wall is so low that heath and bilberry plants have climbed over it from the moor' (p. 205). Even here, the boundary between nature and culture is indistinct and it seems that Cathy cannot be said finally to belong to either.

6. The Lovers

In contrasting the impact of Wuthering Heights with the impact of Thrushcross Grange on the lives of the characters in the novel, we have not yet done justice to the nature of their personal involvements with each other. After all, Cathy does not die because of a conflict of ideologies. She dies because that is the only sure way of renewing her bond with Heathcliff. The absoluteness of their love is such that anything is worth sacrificing for it; in the popular imagination, that is what the novel is about. This section of the study will try to determine the meaning of the lovers' relationship.

Cathy's own version of her childhood relationship with Heathcliff shows that their attachment grows out of the pressure exerted by others to force them apart. This decisive circumstance is made apparent in the very first fragment of her diary we are enabled to see. Lockwood spots a caricature of Joseph, and then reads:

'An awful Sunday!' commenced the paragraph beneath. 'I wish my father were back again. Hindley is a detestable substitute – his conduct to Heathcliff is atrocious – H. and I are going to rebel – we took our initiatory step this evening.' (p. 62)

The more savagery Hindley employs in trying to accomplish his aim, the deeper Cathy's feelings for Heathcliff become. The extraordinary unity of the two children, and their division from the society of others, is signalled by the way that they use clothes, not to advertise singleness, but to express their togetherness in opposition to all others. On the 'awful Sunday' just mentioned, Cathy fastens their pinafores together to make a single curtain for their hiding place under the arch of the dresser. This antisocial act is situated in the place from which, many years later, the untamed violence of the bitch pointer will emerge. Later the same day, they escape under cover of the dairy woman's cloak for their scamper on the moors in the rain. In symbolic terms, they exchange the shelter of civilization for the tumultuous state of nature.

The rebelliousness of the children is augmented by a native vivacity on Cathy's part. Clearly, she would have been disruptive and irrepressible, even if Heathcliff had never come on to the scene. But their very banding together presents their elders with a potential means of bringing them under control: 'The greatest punishment we could invent for her was to keep her separate from him' (p. 83); the fact that this punishment does not always fit the crime is likely to diminish the children's respect for authority. As her father gets older, he also gets contradictory, and Cathy is often at a loss to comprehend the reason for his reproofs:

After behaving as badly as possible all day, she sometimes came fondling to make it up at night.

'Nay, Cathy,' the old man would say, 'I cannot love thee; thou'rt worse than thy brother. Go, say thy prayers, child, and ask God's pardon. I doubt thy mother and I must rue that we ever reared thee!' (p. 84)

To be condemned as worse than Hindley makes Cathy feel that she is rejected indiscriminately, and this helps to make her immune to the demands of conventional morality. Her father's rebuff includes an injunction to her to say her prayers, and this would remind her of Joseph's ascendancy. Joseph is the spokesman of the orthodoxy in the name of which Cathy and Heathcliff are punished; his own self-righteousness is only equalled by the strictness and vindictiveness of his treatment of the children. The negative extent of his influence is such that, already by the time of old Earnshaw's death, the children's idea of the afterlife has little to do with the heaven of orthodox religion: 'no parson in the world ever pictured heaven so beautifully as they did, in their innocent talk' (p. 85). Nelly is indulging what she takes to be mere childishness, but the fact is, if the children do not comply with the tenets of orthodox morality and religion they must pay a penalty for it. In Joseph's view, you are either one of the elect, or you are damned; and the children show their contempt for this narrow-mindedness by hurling into the dog-kennel both *The Helmet of Salvation* and *The Broad Way to Destruction* – they refuse to accept that these are the only alternatives.

After Earnshaw's death, Hindley deprives Heathcliff of the instructions of the curate, thus putting the process of alienation on to a systematic basis. What started from an antipathy towards the conventions of society is turned into an enforced exclusion on cultural grounds. Heathcliff's view of his own childhood is summed up by implication when he speculates about the set-up at Thrushcross Grange:

'Cathy and I escaped from the wash-house to have a ramble at liberty, and getting a glimpse of the Grange lights, we thought we would just go and see whether the Lintons passed their Sunday evenings standing shivering in corners, while their father and mother sat eating and drinking, and singing and laughing, and burning their eyes out before the fire. Do you think they do? Or reading sermons, and being catechised by their man-servant, and set to learn a column of Scripture names, if they don't answer properly?' (p. 88)

The love between Cathy and Heathcliff comes to be defined with reference to nature largely because the restrictive codes of the family, society and religion do not allow it any other sphere in which to operate. We need to remember that this is the context of their love when we try to make sense of Cathy's decision to marry Edgar.

The reasons she gives for choosing to marry Edgar are that he is handsome, young, cheerful, rich, and in love with her. Such a combination, she says, is what makes her '"love the ground under his feet, and the air over his head, and everything he touches, and every word he says – I love all his looks and all his actions, and him entirely, and altogether. There now!"' (pp. 118–19). Such a string of clichés is hardly expressive of genuine feeling, as Nelly is quick to perceive. A few questions from her reveal the emptiness of Cathy's claims; more – Cathy is forced to admit that the only thing that stops her from actually hating Edgar is his presentability. However, she insists, presentability is all-important. Nelly ceases to take her seriously at this point and is ready to conclude the discussion. Cathy proclaims self-satisfaction at her choice, yet she is unable to relax without Nelly's approval of it. It is plain that she senses the wrong she does in accepting Edgar's proposal, and only wants Nelly to confirm her doubts. It must be remembered that the clinching factor in her going ahead with the marriage is Heathcliff's disappearance – in the middle of this very debate.

When Nelly forces her to spell out the cause of her agitation, Cathy immediately adopts a more passionate note, striking her body to direct attention to the state of her soul. Nelly soon realizes the unorthodox trend of her thoughts and nervously tries to prevent her account of a dream she has had. But Cathy, who does not know that Heathcliff is listening, recounts both the dream and her own interpretation of it:

'I was only going to say that heaven did not seem to be my home; and I broke my heart with weeping to come back to earth; and the angels were so angry that they flung me out, into the middle of the heath on the top of Wuthering Heights, where I woke sobbing for joy. That will do to explain my secret, as well as the other. I've no more business to marry Edgar Linton than I have to be in heaven; and if the wicked man in there had not brought Heathcliff so low, I shouldn't have thought of it. It would degrade me to marry Heathcliff, now; so he shall never know how I love him; and that, not because he's handsome, Nelly, but because he's more myself than I am. Whatever our souls are made of, his and mine are the same, and Linton's is as different as a moonbeam from lightning, or frost from fire.' (pp. 120–121)

It comes as no surprise that Cathy should find the conventional notion of heaven far inferior to Wuthering Heights; we know already how she and Heathcliff have been excluded from the universe of conventional morality – almost literally flung out by the angels. What she is also saying is that she and Heathcliff love each other to the extent of un-animity, but that they are bound to be separated to the degree that it is impossible to ignore the reality of social divisions. Clearly, she does not mean to abandon Heathcliff, but the simple fact is, once she has started to think in terms of Heathcliff's being 'degraded', they are lost – their relationship can never be the same. This, at least, is the judgement of Heathcliff, who walks out at about this point. His exit means that he does not hear Cathy's moving, but comparatively useless, spiritual commitment to him. The pathetic side of Cathy's analysis of the problem is her imagining that marriage to Edgar will not involve severance from Heathcliff. This shows such an extraordinary ignorance of reality that Nelly is to blame for not trying to correct it. Cathy even says that she would forget the idea of marrying Edgar if it meant the loss of Heathcliff, and she supposes that her future husband will 'simply shake off his antipathy, and tolerate him' (p. 122). Is it simply appalling naïvety, or an appalling depth of self-deception that makes her so confident that Edgar will warm to Heathcliff once he has discovered the true nature of his wife's feelings for a man he himself has always detested? Cathy's attempts to rationalize her decision – 'if I marry Linton, I can aid Heathcliff to rise, and place him out of my brother's power' (p. 122) – are incon-ceivably flimsy when compared with the force that she brings to the characterization of her bond with Heathcliff – which ought to reverse her decision. This famous speech is already an elegy for the simple and uncorrupted stage of their love:

'I cannot express it; but surely you and everybody have a notion that there is, or should be an existence of yours beyond you. What were the use of my creation if I were entirely contained here? My great miseries in this world have been Heath-cliff's miseries, and I watched and felt each from the beginning; my great thought in living is himself. If all else perished, and *he* remained, I should still continue to be; and if all else remained, and he were annihilated, the universe would turn to a mighty stranger. I should not seem a part of it. My love for Linton is like the foliage in the woods. Time will change it, I'm well aware, as winter changes the trees. My love for Heathcliff resembles the eternal rocks beneath – a source of little visible delight, but necessary. Nelly, I *am* Heathcliff – he's always, always in my mind – not as a pleasure, any more than I am always a pleasure to myself – but as my own being – so, don't talk of our separation again – it is impracticable; and –' (p. 122)

Here, the childish bond forged in adversity becomes something much more mysterious, something unfathomable in terms of ordinary human relationships. However, as Terry Eagleton has pointed out, Cathy's declaration of absolute oneness with Heathcliff is actually *mystifying* a concrete situation in which a total commitment to him is still only a commitment on one level. She describes her identity with him as a timeless one; it is not bound by the usual constraints of mortal life. In other words, if their love survives on some unearthly plane, entirely unaffected by whatever happens in temporal life, then this leaves Cathy free to marry Edgar without fear of endangering the purity of her bond with Heathcliff. If she exalts Heathcliff to an immaterial state of being indistinguishable from hers, it is at the cost of denying him any sort of congress with her material, social self. This is not to suggest that her pledge is in any way specious – so much of the novel testifies to the wholeheartedness of her love. But it is worth mentioning at this point how foreign the idea is to Heathcliff, whose expectations for their relationship are much more down-to-earth, and to that extent much more frustrated.[25]

Cathy's great vow is not usually regarded so sceptically, probably because her division of experience into real and ideal compartments is nearly lost under the cover of analogies which do not distinguish between the tangible and intangible: 'My love for Linton is like the foliage in the woods . . . My love for Heathcliff resembles the eternal rocks beneath . . .' Here, the vivid terms of comparison (which are *only* comparisons) seem to bring both relationships into the physical universe where, to be strictly accurate, both do not belong. The point is, the reader is more likely to remember the physical images than the abstract idea which the images do not go straight to the heart of. It is true that one simile refers to something organic (foliage), and the other to something inorganic (rock), but the distinction this creates is less powerful than the sense of an overall category (nature) into which both fall. And differentiating between Cathy's interest in Edgar and her interest in Heathcliff in terms of competition rather than of mutual irrelevance becomes something of a habit when we are offered several other pairs of images besides this one: 'The contrast resembled what you see in exchanging a bleak, hilly, coal country for a beautiful fertile valley' (p. 110); 'It was not the thorn bending to the honeysuckles, but the honeysuckles embracing the thorn' (p. 131); 'your veins are full of ice-water – but mine are boiling' (p. 156). The first two pairs of opposites work through contrasts of hard and soft, barren and fertile, but the third contrast is more elemental; it reminds us of Cathy's linking Edgar with 'moonbeam' or 'frost', and herself and Heathcliff with 'lightning' or 'fire'. Here, a picturesque sterility (the *opposite* of fertile) is attributed to Edgar, while a destructive intensity is, more familiarly, assigned to the lovers. The breaking of the pattern should make us beware. Generally, Edgar stands for culture against nature; when he is characterized by a natural image, this is always in opposition to another natural image referring to the lovers. Equally, natural imagery is most often used to convey something about Heathcliff, or about the nature of his relationship with Cathy – as it is on the night that he leaves the Heights and a tumult in nature occurs.

Cathy does not realize that Heathcliff is listening when she delivers her confession to Nelly about the true character of her feelings for him; neither does she realize the damage being caused by Heathcliff's hearing only a part of her prolonged outburst. When Nelly reveals – much too late – what is the case, Cathy's immediate reaction demonstrates how cut off she and Heathcliff have become from ordinary, human concerns: 'She jumped up in a fine fright – flung Hareton on to the settle, and ran to seek for her friend herself' (p. 123). Her utter negligence of a child's welfare calls into question the value of her intense concern, at the same time, for Heathcliff and for what he may be feeling. The destructive edge which surrounds the manifestations of their love is not only fatal to themselves but potentially damaging to others. Their obliviousness to ordinary human decency is most powerfully articulated by Heathcliff on the much later occasion of his attempt to visit the dying Cathy. He is opposed by Nelly, who implicitly condemns his own reckless passion by stressing the merits of Edgar's affection, based as it is upon *duty*, *humanity*, *pity* and *charity*. The reader is already aware of how totally inapplicable such an appeal is in the context of the terms with which the lovers have always expressed themselves; but the withering scorn which Heathcliff shows for these basic human values is quite breathtaking. Does this mean that Heathcliff is evil? Not necessarily, because ideas like 'pity' and 'humanity' have come to be associated in his mind with intolerable hypocrisy. If Cathy is being attended out of 'duty' or 'charity', what that means to Heathcliff is that she is 'in hell'. The lovers' contempt for conventional morality is partly due to a measure of inhumanity on their part, but is also partly due to the fact that the language of conventional morality simply does not mean what it says.

Their inhumanity is most consistently hinted at in their apparent indifference to physical discomfort and even severe pain. The idea that physical suffering may count as nothing beside mental anguish is not all that remarkable, but in the case of Cathy and Heathcliff it is almost as if their existence in corporeal form is irrelevant. It seems significant that Heathcliff talks of 'haunting' Cathy even before her death, and that she 'haunts' him after it. In this respect, their relationship *does* seem to have its being in some supernatural context. But there is a paradox: the idea that they may be present to each other in disembodied states is encouraged by the frequency of occasions on which they are physically ferocious towards themselves and each other. In their last scene together while both are still alive, we seem to be witnessing a moment in which their love is actually trying to break through the physical obstacles of skin and bone:

'Don't torture me till I'm as mad as yourself,' cried he, wrenching his head free, and grinding his teeth.
   The two, to a cool spectator, made a strange and fearful picture. Well might Catherine deem that heaven would be a land of exile to her, unless, with her mortal body, she cast away her mortal character also. Her present countenance had a wild vindictiveness in its white cheek, and a bloodless lip, and scintillating eye; and she retained, in her closed fingers, a portion of the locks she had been grasping. As to her companion, while raising himself with one hand, he had taken her arm with the other; and so inadequate was his stock of gentleness to the requirements of her condition, that on his letting go, I saw four distinct impressions left blue in the colourless skin. (p. 195)

This is an extraordinary moment because it seems to lend force to Cathy's belief that nothing can part her from Heathcliff, not even their separation into different bodies. But while their unanimity is so intense that they do not feel what their bodies are suffering, the visible evidence of physical damage is none the less there as a poignant reminder of just how real the barriers between them are. The 'strangeness' of the situation is such that we cannot translate it into easily understandable terms; what Heathcliff feels on Cathy's behalf is immense, but we hesitate to call it something like 'compassion', when even his tears appear to be self-contradictory: 'they burned with anguish, they did not melt'. (Remember that Heathcliff is like 'fire', Edgar like 'ice'.) The lovers' bodies do not obey the usual rules; Cathy ceases to pay much attention to material existence once she has realized that it does not contain her real 'home'. For some time before her death, she wears a vague and distant look 'which expressed no recognition of material things either by ear or eye' (p. 193). She describes her own body as a 'shattered prison' (p. 196) against whose walls she is straining for a chance to escape. The sheer impossibility of their love, and their defiance of that impossibility, are alike expressed in terms of massive physical strain; their last embrace (this side of the grave) has an almost murderous aspect:

His eyes wide, and wet, at last, flashed fiercely on her; his breast heaved convulsively. An instant they held asunder; and then how they met I hardly saw, but

Catherine made a spring, and he caught her, and they were locked in an embrace from which I thought my mistress would never be released alive. In fact, to my eyes, she seemed directly insensible. He flung himself into the nearest seat, and on my approaching hurriedly to ascertain if she had fainted, he gnashed at me, and foamed like a mad dog, and gathered her to him with greedy jealousy. I did not feel as if I were in the company of a creature of my own species; it appeared that he would not understand, though I spoke to him; so, I stood off, and held my tongue, in great perplexity. (p. 197)

It is as if the two lovers were expending, by means of offensive vigour, all the energy that has been prevented from taking a sexual form. It is no wonder that their behaviour is beyond Nelly's comprehension, since in this, as in other respects, it is beyond her experience. She is right to think of Heathcliff as foreign to her species; in his closeness to Cathy he is inhuman, but not simply in the pejorative sense that Nelly intends. He is not inhuman in a brutish way so much as in his total disregard for the normal categories of human thought and feeling. The accusations he now levels at Cathy show a sweeping independence of conventional morality and religion, and a corresponding degree of subjection to the words and actions of the woman he loves (he remembers her casting him off as 'degraded'): 'Because misery, and degradation, and death, and nothing that God or Satan could inflict would have parted us, *you*, of your own will, did it' (p. 197). The great religious concepts mean nothing except with regard to the state of their relationship; hell and heaven are defined purely in terms of being separated from Cathy, or being together with her. It is hardly consoling that Heathcliff chooses this moment to reciprocate Cathy's great exclamation of unity: '"Catherine, you know that I could as soon forget you, as my existence!"' (p. 196). By this time, she has found that the only way of fulfilling the spirit of her commitment to Heathcliff is by dying and so releasing herself from the clutches of everything except love for him. His conception of their togetherness is much more bound by an awareness of physical existence, as his subsequent fascination with the state of her corpse, and his need to see and hear the spirit of Cathy, will reveal.

Either way, Nelly is far wide of the mark in her contemplation of the dead Cathy. As she gazes on 'that untroubled image of Divine rest' (p. 201) she echoes the words that Cathy had uttered only a few hours before – '"I shall be incomparably beyond and above you all"' (p. 197) – but misconstrues them to mean that 'her spirit is at home with God!' (p. 201). Cathy's last thoughts had stopped far short of anticipating any union with God, and Nelly's little bit of commentary shows a total misunderstanding, not only of her words, but of the whole tenor of her life. This is confirmed by Heathcliff's exasperation with Nelly when she brings him the news of Cathy's death; Nelly finds him waiting in the park,

> leant against an old ash tree, his hat off, and his hair soaked with the dew that had gathered on the budded branches, and fell pattering round him. He had been standing a long time in that position, for I saw a pair of ousels passing and repassing, scarcely three feet from him, busy in building their nest, and regarding his proximity no more than that of a piece of timber. (pp. 202–3)

For the moment, Heathcliff resembles a natural object more than a human being. If we remember Cathy's anticipation that her death would release her into an existence where she would be at one with elemental forces, then it seems crucial that at this very moment, just after her death, Heathcliff should appear to possess the impersonality of nature. Nelly tells him what has happened, not without distress, but also without being able to stop herself from moralizing on the state of Cathy's soul. Heathcliff disparages her remarks, sneering and 'defying, meanwhile, my sympathy with an unflinching, ferocious stare' (p. 203). What Nelly calls 'sympathy' has the outward form of a glib piety, and Heathcliff is defying it because in his view Nelly has a limited understanding of what has taken place; her view is distorted by conventional assumptions. His hardness is a deliberately simulated hardness, and what his behaviour shows is a very deep grief at the same time as a belligerent concealment of that grief. The reader can perceive this, but it is successfully concealed from Nelly, who patronizingly registers the fact that he gets somewhat close to having, if not actually having, authentic human feelings.

Nelly has no warrant for her revision of Cathy's final moments. She probably means to comfort Heathcliff by adding to what we already know the assurance that 'her latest ideas wandered back to pleasant early days. Her life closed in a gentle dream' (p. 204). But this would suggest to Heathcliff that Cathy was reconciled to separation from him, and he is almost driven senseless by the possibility. While still coherent, he prays a blasphemous prayer that Cathy may *not* have rest until he himself is dead, begs her to haunt him, and predicts an existence of living death for himself: 'I *cannot* live without my life! I *cannot* live without my soul!' (p. 204). This done, he relapses into a kind of fit:

> He dashed his head against the knotted trunk; and, lifting up his eyes, howled, not like a man, but like a savage beast getting goaded to death with knives and spears. (p. 204)

This reminds us of the lovers' indifference to bodily pain and underlines their segregation from ordinary humanity. But it also does something else: there is a curious emphasis in the awkward phrasing of the last clause: 'getting goaded.' Heathcliff is not just like a wild animal, he is like a cornered, disadvantaged animal reacting to tormentors. We are reminded that the lovers' faith in each other was born in a spirit of adversity, that it had to fight to survive against every attempt to crush it. Heathcliff's loss of self-control occurs in a moment of tragic defeat – it is a profoundly emotional gesture. Yet Nelly – who is the main interpreter of the action – understands nothing of this: 'It hardly moved my compassion – it appalled me' (p. 204). She is ill-equipped to sympathize with Heathcliff, either on this occasion, or later on, when his undying love for Cathy strikes her as a repugnant obsession.

This makes it all the more pathetic when, eighteen years later, Heathcliff turns to Nelly as the only one who can begin to comprehend his motive in trying to disinter Cathy. This grotesquely touching episode produces so much elation in him that he has to communicate his joy. He tells of hearing a sigh above the grave, and of sensing '"warm breath . . . displacing the sleet-laden wind"' (p. 320). He is absolutely certain of Cathy's presence, without being gratified by a single glimpse: '"I could *almost* see her, and yet I *could not*!"' (p. 321). After being haunted by her memory for eighteen years, he is still deriving strength from this virtual encounter with his 'spectre of a hope' (p. 321). Nelly maintains a frigid silence throughout the greater part of his narrative, but the insight it affords into years of unremitting anguish and unbearable loneliness is likely to renew the reader's sympathy for the ever more 'inhuman' Heathcliff.

The whole period of time between Cathy's death and his own is a long drawn out process of mortification. Heathcliff has to remind himself to eat and drink, to breathe and even to compel his heart to beat, as if his real self were only with difficulty human. Whenever stress is laid upon his bodily functions, these are depicted as paradoxical processes which should be inimical to life: 'his eyes rained down tears among the ashes, and he drew his breath in suffocating sighs' (p. 216). His fixation is able to contradict the evidence of all his senses, and he sees, hears, thinks and feels the presence of Cathy in absolutely everything:

'I cannot look down to this floor, but her features are shaped on the flags! In every cloud, in every tree – filling the air at night, and caught by glimpses in every object, by day I am surrounded with her image! The most ordinary faces of men, and women – my own features mock me with a resemblance. The entire world is a dreadful collection of memoranda that she did exist, and that I have lost her!' (p. 353)

This is the major statement on Heathcliff's part to the effect that he and Cathy hardly exist in human form but are rather immanent in the moors and the Heights. He can see Cathy even in his own features, at the same time as his own features are displaced elsewhere:

'Well, Hareton's aspect was the ghost of my immortal love, of my wild endeavours to hold my right, my degradation, my pride, my happiness, and my anguish –' (p. 354)

This spontaneous effort to epitomize his love for Cathy involves a hopeless, intolerable compound of feelings and experiences which could never combine themselves into a recognizably human form. Small wonder that the true nature of Heathcliff's agony goes unrecognized by the other characters. As Nelly says, 'not a soul, from his general bearing, would have conjectured the fact' (p. 355). He has been universally condemned for his inhumanity, because this is more visible than the suffering that will always have been there, even when not made apparent.

Well before his death, Heathcliff has become radically alien and unassimilable to the society of others. He eats only once every twenty-four hours, but does not feel hunger. He spends as much time as possible in the room with the window where Lockwood had had his dream encounter with Cathy's spirit. And he is overwhelmed by hallucinations, seeing more and more over the threshold into another world, and having less and less attachment to this one:

Now, I perceived he was not looking at the wall, for when I regarded him alone, it seemed, exactly, that he gazed at something within two yards distance. And, whatever it was, it communicated, apparently, both pleasure and pain, in exquisite extremes; at least, the anguished, yet raptured expression of his countenance suggested that idea. (p. 361)

Nelly tries to shake off the suspicion that there is something supernatural in all this, but the kind of supernaturalism she has in mind is that of traditional folklore. The author supplies a more interesting possibility in a simile which strikes us at once as being oddly literary for Nelly: Heathcliff's frame is said to shiver, 'not as one shivers with chill or weakness, but as a tight-stretched cord vibrates – a strong thrilling, rather than trembling' (p. 358). Nelly could not know it, but Brontë would hardly be unaware of the connotations of this standard Romantic figure. It suggests a condition in which the self is influenced by an ideal force – that breath of being which is beyond the usual infections of human life, moral and physical. Heathcliff dies without accepting the judgement of men, or the judgement of God. He never feels remorse for any of his actions: '"as to repenting of my injustices, I've done no injustice, and I repent of nothing"' (p. 363). And his last instructions to the bewildered Nelly show an insurmountable indifference to orthodox Christianity '"No minister need come; nor need anything be said over me – I tell you, I have nearly attained *my* heaven; and that of others is altogether unvalued, and uncoveted by me!"' (p. 363)

The lovers' exemption from the world of commonly held beliefs is well attested to; but a careful sifting of the evidence suggests that it does not mean the same to Heathcliff as it does to Cathy. What is the significance of Cathy's appearing to Lockwood in the form of a child? This is the only image we have of her after death, because no matter how hard he tries, Heathcliff fails to actually *see* the spirit that is tormenting him. The image of the child may lend support to the idea that in marrying the weak and ineffectual Edgar, rather than the powerful and vigorous Heathcliff, Cathy is trying to escape the demands of adult sexuality. Her frequent recourse to physical violence, not only towards Heathcliff and herself, but also in sudden bouts of malice against the servants, might be an index of the strain involved in trying to keep her sexual life in a state of total eclipse. It has been argued that the emotional register of the entire novel is that of hysterical children.[26] It may be so, partly because all the parental figures in the novel (including their substitute, Nelly Dean) prove to be untrustworthy. It may equally well be that Cathy (whose words and actions dictate the course of Heathcliff's entire life) is simply unable to mature. In this connection, the feminist critics Gilbert and Gubar have drawn attention to her relationship with her substitute parents Hindley and Frances, who are resented as much as step-parents in fairy tales. One important aspect of the child Cathy's antagonism is the fact that Hindley and Frances are impossible to ignore as sexual beings: 'there they were, like two babies, kissing and talking nonsense by the hour – foolish palaver that we should be ashamed of' (p. 63). Cathy's breezy contempt on her own and Heathcliff's behalf only serves to hide a deeper unease, because Hindley is also the bane of their lives. Just at the time when she is discovering her own sexual identity, Cathy is presented with an example of sexual activity which seems, because of the persons involved, to align it with selfish, violent and incomprehensible behaviour. Her refusal to cooperate with what Hindley and Frances represent, while it is aggravating to them, is much more damaging to Heathcliff in the long run. When Frances dies because of something connected with sex (she has just given birth to Hareton) it seems to set the seal on Cathy's rejection of womanhood; she would rather be a lady, with all the detachment from strong feeling and physicality that that seems to imply.[27]

At this point, we ought to remember how badly she fails in this ambition. No matter what her initial promptings might be to try to absorb Heathcliff into herself, and so defuse in him what she cannot cope with, their relationship comes to mean much more. Both the kind and the degree of intensity which they bring to their passion make it impossible to sustain in any of the given social roles. This turns it into a powerful form of social criticism which puts to the test the values of those who are the open or covert adversaries of their love. Because they refuse to adopt the available language of sublimity, they are exiled into the non-human worlds of nature and death. The selflessness involved in their giving themselves up to the hope of togetherness in both these contexts offers a stark contrast to the conventional modes of affection, which never entirely manage to divorce themselves from a language of self-interest. The impersonality of their love gives it an unprecedented scale and grandeur, but at the same time makes it alienating to outsiders. Those outsiders are revealed as the props and stays of a culture which cannot afford to dispense with its opposition to fellow-feeling. Although their love is unable to realize itself in social and historical terms, Cathy and Heathcliff present the other characters – especially Nelly and Lockwood – and the reader, with an everlasting problem of how to make sense of their lives. The inability to pin down the meaning of their relationship, or even to find the right framework for thinking about it, persists as a constant source of friction with social, moral and religous norms.

7. Heathcliff: Devil or Man?

When Isabella is imprisoned by Heathcliff at Wuthering Heights, she sends a letter to Nelly which includes the question, '"Is Mr Heathcliff a man? If so, is he mad? And if not, is he a devil?"' (p. 173). Since she had started off in the belief that he was something akin to a Byronic hero, her discovery of his real nature might well lead her to this dramatic cynicism. She is the last person who could ever be objective about him – her blind love is changed into blind hatred literally overnight. But Isabella is not alone in this feeling of awe and loathing of Heathcliff. Nearly every character in the novel (including Cathy herself) asks the same question about him. In trying to establish the degree to which he might be 'devilish', we have to distinguish between the evidence of his own actions, and the prejudices of those for whom his very existence represents a greater or lesser threat. We already know, from the previous section, how badly he fits into the categories of thought and evaluation which are in use at both the Heights and the Grange. We have to ask ourselves whether there are any occasions on which he is accused of being a devil simply because his accuser does not know what else to call him; and whether there are other occasions on which his behaviour really does merit the term.

When we first meet him at the start of the book, he does not have much longer to live. He has already committed most of the acts which the other characters will describe as 'devilish'. Lockwood has never met him before, and has to judge him by appearances. What he chiefly notes is extreme unfriendliness, and a peculiar relish for the discomfort of others. There is nothing expressly devilish about Heathcliff, except a stray 'diabolical sneer'. Lockwood soon learns that appearances are not only deceptive, but also contradictory in Heathcliff's case: 'He is a dark skinned gypsy, in aspect, in dress, and manners a gentleman' (p. 47). The simultaneous presence of contrasts allows scope for divergent, even conflicting assessments of Heathcliff's personality. Gypsies are, of course, in permanent exile from society, the unreclaimed outsiders of western civilization. Lockwood notices something else untamed about Heathcliff, his momentary identification with the bestial ferocity of his dogs. But apart from this, there is nothing to suggest that he belongs to another species, as Nelly is later to suspect, apart from his feat of almost supernatural strength in wrenching open the soldered window of Cathy's room. To be sure, the miserable hostility with which the inmates of Wuthering Heights regard each other is traceable to Heathcliff's influence, and there are hints of mental, if not actually physical, cruelty on his part, as well as clear signs of intolerance. But the dominant impression we receive of him is of his elusive quality, his paradoxical behaviour, his unaccountable harshness towards those in his charge, and his unexplained tenderness towards the invisible Cathy.

What is particularly interesting at this early stage is the fuss with which another character altogether is charged with devilishness. Joseph accuses the younger Catherine of practising witchcraft, and she plays up to the accusation, acting out a little scene in which she appears as a parodic version of the traditional witch. The whole point about the episode is that Joseph takes her seriously; what is meant to be a caricature of evil is mistaken for the genuine article. If Joseph can be so wrong about her, what makes him so right about Heathcliff? Joseph is the major influence on the vocabulary of moral condemnation in use at the Heights. It is too much to say that where he leads, the rest follow, but it is instructive to remember that his bigotry is opposed only by Heathcliff and Cathy; and to a much lesser extent by the younger Catherine.

Our major source of information about Heathcliff is, of course, the redoubtable Nelly, with her strong urge to conform. Her explanation of how he goes from bad to worse has to surmount the fact of her own unreasonable antipathy towards him as a child. The fact that he comes into the story and into the lives of the other characters as a human mystery, in the sense that his parental origins are completely unknown, makes him both slightly more and slightly less than human for them. Old Earnshaw presents him in relatively grandiose terms: '"See here, wife; I was never so beaten with anything in my life; but you must e'en take it as a gift of God; though it's as dark almost as if it came from the devil"' (p. 77). From the moment of his first appearance, then, he is given a dual aspect; what may be angelic to some, may appear devilish to others. The majority opinion favours the latter view, but old Earnshaw starts off by insisting otherwise: you *must* think of the child as heaven-sent. On closer acquaintance, Heathcliff appears to sustain the paradox of his introduction: 'he was as uncomplaining as a lamb, though hardness, not gentleness, made him give little trouble' (p. 79). The boy's attitude is understandable in one who has been abandoned on the streets of Liverpool, but the country-bred Nelly can only partly understand that; she tries to make sense of his hardness in conventional terms which refer it to his moral state instead of his social condition. From a Christian point of view, a hard lamb is a contradiction in terms.

Nelly and the others find it easy to reject the idea that Heathcliff is a blessing in disguise because his language – 'some gibberish that nobody could understand' – is outlandish, even threatening, to the members of a small, isolated community. Nelly admits to having been frightened, while Mrs Earnshaw's desire to '"fling it out of doors"' curiously anticipates Mrs Linton's abhorrence of Heathcliff on linguistic grounds. In their own language, they marginalize the unwelcome child as 'it' and 'thing'. Nelly is charged with looking after him, to the extent of washing and clothing him and putting him to sleep with the other children. But she fails even in this, leaving him to spend the night on the landing of the stairs. As a result, old Earnshaw throws her out for nothing less than 'inhumanity' – which is a remarkable inversion of her future relation to Heathcliff. By the time of her return, Heathcliff has already begun his alliance with Cathy, while Hindley has set the pattern of a life-long rivalry. Nelly joins with Hindley in a campaign of hatred and violence, joining her pinches to his blows, and in this she is not only inhumane but also dishonest, since she must have expressed remorse for her conduct to old Earnshaw. Heathcliff weathers through, thanks largely to the death of Mrs Earnshaw, which reduces the amount of opposition to him. With the balance of power affected in this way, Nelly grudgingly transfers her loyalty from Hindley to Heathcliff. She admits that, after having nursed Heathcliff – rather dispassionately – through a serious illness, the commendations of the doctor made her soften 'towards the being by whose means I earned them'. She could not warm to him personally. In fact she admits to taking steps to hide the amount of injuries which he receives from Hindley, which suggests that she has a residual emotional commitment to Hindley, and that her association with Heathcliff is merely expedient. In his deepening isolation, Hindley understandably grows more bitter and behaves more desperately, as Nelly shows in her 'instance' of the state of affairs:

As an instance, I remember Mr Earnshaw once bought a couple of colts at the parish fair, and gave the lads each one. Heathcliff took the handsomest, but it soon fell lame, and when he discovered it, he said to Hindley,

'You must exchange horses with me; I don't like mine, and if you won't I shall tell your father of the three thrashings you've given me this week, and show him my arm, which is black to the shoulder'.

Hindley put out his tongue, and cuffed him over the ears.

'You'd better do it at once,' he persisted, escaping to the porch (they were in the stable); 'you will have to, and if I speak of these blows, you'll get them again with interest.'

'Off, dog!' cried Hindley, threatening him with an iron weight, used for weighing potatoes and hay.

'Throw it,' he replied, standing still, 'and then I'll tell how you boasted that you would turn me out of doors as soon as he died, and see whether he will not turn you out directly.'

Hindley threw it, hitting him on the breast, and down he fell, but staggered up immediately, breathless and white, and had not I prevented it, he would have gone just so to the master, and got full revenge by letting his condition plead for him, intimating who had caused it.

'Take my colt, gipsy then!' said young Earnshaw, 'And I pray that he may break your neck, take him, and be damned, you beggarly interloper! and wheedle my father out of all he has, only, afterwards, show him what you are, imp of Satan – And take that, I hope he'll kick out your brains!'

Heathcliff had gone to loose the beast, and shift it to his own stall – He was passing behind it, when Hindley finished his speech by knocking him under its feet, and without stopping to examine whether his hopes were fulfilled, ran away as fast as he could.

I was surprised to witness how coolly the child gathered himself up, and went on with his intention, exchanging saddles and all; and then sitting down on a bundle of hay to overcome the qualm which the violent blow occasioned, before he entered the house.

I persuaded him easily to let me lay the blame of his bruises on the horse; he minded little what tale was told since he had what he wanted. He complained so seldom, indeed, of such stirs as these, that I really thought him not vindictive – I was deceived, completely, as you will hear. (pp. 80–81)

What this extensive quotation reveals is Nelly's suspicion of something unnatural, perhaps even supernatural, in a child who can remain unperturbed by a scene of violent altercation. She suggests that he was hiding what he really felt, that he was concealing from those around him a purpose of revenge. She insinuates that vindictiveness was always in his nature. But it is more likely that his passive resistance is only changed into an active desire for revenge by events subsequent to this. Nelly is evidently skilful at telling falsehoods – 'I persuaded him easily to let me lay the blame of his bruises on the horse' – which does not enhance her reliability as a narrator. And she is unable to conceal her feeling that Hindley is justified in taking a stand against the 'beggarly interloper'; she attributes the speech in which Heathcliff is accused of wanting to deprive the Earnshaws of their property, not to Hindley (which is what she usually does) but to 'young Earnshaw', thus emphasizing his rights as heir to the property.

Heathcliff's behaviour is decidedly immoral, but we have to remember that he has had to survive the persecutions of Hindley ever since his arrival. Since Hindley was already fourteen at that time, while Heathcliff was only 'big enough both to walk and talk', his only hope of fending for himself would be through the use of his wits. Specifically, he would have to turn his only weapon – the affection of old Earnshaw – to every possible advantage. We cannot help noticing how unimpassioned and perfunctory his blackmail of Hindley is.

Hindley's behaviour is pathetic and ignoble. His attempts to injure Heathcliff (with the iron weight and the horse) are serious ones; and he is habitually brutal, as the series of bruises on Heathcliff's arm makes clear. The latter is hardly likely to develop a sense of fair play when nearly every day brings such a physical ordeal. Hindley's tireless attempts to oppress Heathcliff are comprehensible to the extent that he represents a threat to Hindley's own position as heir to the property; he has already supplanted Hindley in the affections of his own father. Nelly is initially hostile to the newcomer because he threatens to displace her from her position as the family's most favoured dependent. She is soon made to realize that she must put up with this or clear out altogether. Cathy is free to respond to Heathcliff without prejudice, partly because her own position as daughter of the family means that she has nothing to lose from his presence at the Heights. In fact, the reverse is partly the case, since his presence gives her a sphere of influence where none had existed before.

Almost the last thing that Hindley does in this episode is to label Heathcliff an 'imp of Satan', whether because of his unnatural powers of endurance, or because of his cunning. This view of Heathcliff as satanic is one that Nelly tentatively subscribes to, partly because she tends to identify with the cause of Hindley rather than that of Heathcliff. She regards the latter's trouble-making propensities as inherent in his character, irrespective of the atmosphere of conflict which he has had to grow up in; thus, on his return from the first visit to the Grange, she scolds him with being 'incurable'. Even when she offers him advice on how to improve his appearance, so as to be able to compete with Edgar for Cathy's favours, she does so in terms which suggest how radical and even wilful she thinks his badness is:

'Come to the glass and I'll let you see what you should wish. Do you mark those two lines between your eyes, and those thick brows, that instead of rising arched, sink in the middle, and that couple of black fiends, so deeply buried, who never open their windows boldly, but lurk glinting under them, like devil's spies? Wish and learn to smooth away the surly wrinkles, to raise your lids frankly, and change the fiends to confident, innocent angels, suspecting and doubting nothing; and always seeing friends where they are not sure of foes . . .' (p. 97)

What Nelly is doing here is to link fiendishness, or devilishness, with a lack of trust on Heathcliff's part. But what basis does Heathcliff have for trusting anybody, including Cathy at this stage? To begin, suddenly, to trust people as a matter of course would be to contradict the whole of his experience; and so he is forced to remain, in Nelly's eyes, both devilish and incurable. It is only *after* she has made plain her misgivings about his character that she is ready to admit that Hindley's 'bad ways and bad companions formed a pretty example for Catherine and Heathcliff. His treatment of the latter was enough to make a fiend of a saint' (p. 106). She is referring here to the period after the death of Frances, when Hindley's degeneration makes him more callous. But this is long after she has made up her mind about the basis of Heathcliff's fiendishness. He seems most fiendish to the reader once he has replaced his childhood resentments with a grown-up lust for revenge; but what makes him develop from the one to the other? It is interesting that Nelly, after having told Heathcliff to be trustful so that he would lose his frown, manages to smooth away the wrinkles on his brow by quite different means. She plants in him the idea which is to be the germ of his future revenge. She calls attention to his obscure origins, and encourages him to imagine that he might have had noble, rather than humble, parents:

'Who knows, but your father was Emperor of China, and your mother an Indian queen, each of them able to buy up, with one week's income, Wuthering Heights and Thrushcross Grange together? And you were kidnapped by wicked sailors, and brought to England. Were I in your place, I would frame high notions of my birth; and the thoughts of what I was should give me courage and dignity to support the oppressions of a little farmer!' (p. 98)

Heathcliff is noticeably pacified by this train of thought, but it is something that he could not have thought of on his own; his mind simply does not work that way. It is ironically Nelly, who says she was 'completely' deceived about Heathcliff's vindictiveness, who opens his eyes to his only possible chance of defeating both Edgar and Hindley. It is from this moment that we can date the onset of his determination to ruin his enemies. Only a day later, he admits to 'trying to settle how I shall pay Hindley back' (p. 101). Nelly is typically scandalized by such an un-Christian attitude: '"It is for God to punish wicked people; we should learn to forgive"' (p. 101). She forgets how often God has been used by Joseph to sanction the unfair punishments meted out to Cathy and Heathcliff.

Before long, Heathcliff becomes completely unfriended and deprived of culture. And through constant brooding on what seems the only way out of his dilemma, he begins to acquire those characteristics which are to cut him off from the rest of humanity. Nelly recounts an incident in which he saves the life of Hareton by arresting his fall from the top of a flight of stairs:

A miser who has parted with a lucky lottery ticket for five shillings, and finds next day he has lost in the bargain five thousand pounds, could not show a blanker countenance than he did on beholding the figure of Mr Earnshaw above – It expressed, plainer than words could do, the intensest anguish at having made himself the instrument of thwarting his own revenge. (p. 115)

Nelly's simile is apt, first because Heathcliff does actually become a miser in order to secure revenge, and secondly because it associates the acquisition of property with an unnatural degree of enmity, a peculiarly violent form of aggressiveness. Heathcliff can only wreak his revenge by acquiring property and becoming a landlord; his behaviour is only a particularly blatant form of the aggressiveness which must underlie any relationship based on the unequal division of property.

Before we investigate the modulation in Heathcliff's career from that of a victim to that of an oppressor, it is as well to note that both before and after the change in his fortunes, Hindley has as much right to be called 'devilish' as he does. Nelly points out that under Hindley's regime the Heights is an 'infernal' (p. 106) house. His language is as bad as Heathcliff's, if not worse, and his animality is alluded to on almost every occasion he appears. He manhandles Nelly herself, 'pulling me back by the skin of my neck, like a dog' (p. 114) and on one occasion even tries to force a knife down her throat. His vengefulness seems as vehement, if not as sustained, as Heathcliff's: '"I want to kill some of you, I shall have no rest till I do!"' (p. 114). And his treatment of his own son, Hareton, is as unnatural as anything that Heathcliff perpetrates against Linton. It is not surprising that Hareton calls him 'Devil daddy' (p. 148) after exposure to such sentiments as '"he deserves flaying alive for not running to welcome me, and for screaming as if I were a goblin. Unnatural cub, come hither!"' (p. 114). Most significant, perhaps, is the freedom with which Hindley employs the vocabulary of damnation; he speaks of sending his own soul '"to perdition, to punish its maker"' (p. 116), and is an habitual blasphemer.

But Nelly always manages to take Hindley's barbarities in her stride as the actions of a man at the end of his tether, whereas Heathcliff's atrocities always strike her as issuing from an inexhaustible reserve of power. From the moment of his return to the neighbourhood of the Heights and Grange, she becomes much more insistently troubled by an inkling of his supernatural status: '"What!" I cried, uncertain whether to regard him as a worldly visitor, and I raised my hands in amazement. "What! you come back? Is it really you? Is it?"' (p. 132). It is important to recognize that Heathcliff's 'devilish' reputation is built up less by the direct attribution of demonic qualities than by the use of analogies, which do not say that Heathcliff *is* devilish, rather that he inspires as much fear in Nelly, for example, as she would feel *if* she had 'raised a goblin' (p. 149). Similarly, Cathy does not actually say that Heathcliff *is* Satanic when she deprecates the idea of offering Isabella to him as a wife – she says rather that this would be *as bad as* '"offering Satan a lost soul"' (p. 151).

On one point these observers are prepared to be unhesitatingly direct, and that is the question of Heathcliff's ferocity. Cathy warns Isabella that '"he's a fierce, pitiless, wolfish man"' (p. 141) and Heathcliff bears this out with his promise to wrench off Isabella's fingernails '"if they ever menaced me"' (p. 145). He contemplates the possibility of turning her '"blue eyes black, every day or two"' (p. 145) as a routine satisfaction. His desire for revenge has a greater element of gloating in it, now that the means of achieving his desire are closer to hand. But at the same time, we are never allowed to lose sight of the fact that Heathcliff has learned what cruelty is like from being on the receiving end of it. In seeking to oppress those in his power, he is adding one more link to a chain of suffering in which he himself is implicated as victim as well as tyrant. He is never finally accepted in his new position of social superiority, just as he was never completely reduced to the rank of servant. What is most constant in the way that others perceive him, from the beginning of his career to the end, is the radical ambiguity of his nature, which makes it impossible to know exactly what to think of him, or where to place him in the network of social relations. A man whose most salient quality is 'a half-civilized ferocity' (p. 135) is hard to fit in anywhere.

His actions start to assume a much more ruthless character with his abduction of Isabella from the Grange to the Heights. The first thing he does in repayment of her commitment to him is to hang her pet springer, Fanny. This act of needless cruelty is shocking and might even be considered evil by a sensitive young lady from Thrushcross Grange. But at the Heights it would not be thought morally reprehensible; at the start of the novel, Lockwood discovers a heap of dead rabbits, while Isabella herself is later to observe Hareton 'hanging a litter of puppies from a chairback in the doorway' (p. 217). There are no pets at the Heights, where animals have to earn their keep.

Once Isabella is within his power, Heathcliff treats her with an almost mechanical brutality. She responds by declaring him to be '"a lying fiend, a monster, and not a human being!"' (p. 188). But this style of abuse has been learned from Hindley, who can hardly open his mouth without venting his spleen against the '"fiend"', or the '"hellish villain"': '"hell shall have his soul! It will be ten times blacker with that guest than ever it was before!"' (p. 177). In spite of Hindley's rather baroque execrations, and Isabella's furious attempts to make sense of what has happened to her, Heathcliff does nothing convincingly supernatural, unless threatening to tear out Edgar's heart and drink his blood can be counted as such. His own explanation of his conduct and motives shows fewer signs of spiritual evil than of an obdurate efficiency. The most horrifying aspect of his procedure is that law and convention are on his side.

He points out that his marriage to Isabella makes him her '"legal protector"', which gives her no freedom beyond what he allows. He is acting within his rights when he imprisons her at the Heights; he even requires Nelly to bear witness to Isabella's behaviour: '"If you are called upon in a court of law, you'll remember her language"' (p. 188). It is a grotesque irony that Heathcliff should be an embodiment of the law; it is part of his plan to caricature what he sees as the genuinely oppressive nature of legal privileges. When he describes Edgar as having a '"fraternal and magisterial heart"' (p. 188), he is right to stress the paradoxical behaviour of a brother whose love for his sister is wiped out by her negligence of his legal rights over her. Heathcliff's own experience of the Grange has uncovered the violence beneath its propriety, and he may be correct in his surmise that Isabella, having been brought up there, has an innate admiration of brutality. He makes conventional modes of thought work in his favour when he deludes her into '"picturing in me a hero of romance"' (p. 187). His success depends on his ability to exploit the existing inadequacy of a view of life which expects people to behave as they do in novels.

What Heathcliff has done during his absence from the Heights is to acquire just enough culture to be able to use it as a weapon against those who have previously turned it against him. His marriage to Isabella, undertaken solely for material advantage, is intended not only to hit back at Edgar, but also to demonstrate to Cathy what he takes to be the value of her marriage. He is parodying what he understands as her own method of achieving influence and prosperity. Of course, his ambition extends far beyond the exposure of violence and greed in others – he is a man in the grip of an obsession:

'I have no pity! I have no pity! The more the worms writhe, the more I yearn to crush out their entrails! It is a moral teething, and I grind with greater energy, in proportion to the increase of pain'. (p. 189)

What Heathcliff calls a '"moral teething"' involves a gradual erosion of the moral sense, and it is inevitable that he should become corrupted by a process which entraps him as much as his victims. He has acquired even less freedom than he enjoyed as a child, when he was free only in being totally excluded from society; as an adult, he has entered society and discovered that his only freedom therein lies in the enslavement of others. If there is a kind of rough justice in the way that he tricks Edgar and Isabella by turning their own values against them, there is something truly repulsive in the excessive gratification he derives from his power over Isabella, and his determination to conduct. '"experiments on what she could endure"' (p. 188).

Nevertheless, when Isabella finally escapes from his custody, and discloses the extent of her revulsion to Nelly, she uses such extravagant terms (she says that Heathcliff has '"cannibal teeth"', for example) that even Nelly is prompted to contradict her:

'Hush, hush! He's a human being,' I said. 'Be more charitable; there are worse men than he is yet!' (p. 209)

Isabella refers more than once to Heathcliff's '"fiendish prudence"' (the other variant is '"diabolical prudence"') and this seemingly impossible combination of qualities is surely a more adequate reflection of his complicated nature than her usual strain of abuse. She has good enough reasons for wanting to represent him as a monster. The first, which we have already discussed, stems from her having seen in him what she wanted to see – a hero of romance – so that when he failed to match up to that image, she ran to the opposite extreme and condemned him as inhuman. In neither case is her judgement accurate. The second reason why she is unable to understand him, or to imagine what *he* is feeling, is because he has '"destroyed"' her heart. Since her arrival at the Heights he has subjected her to the same brutalizing process of ill-treatment, injustice, oppression, denial of affection and even of basic human rights, that he himself was subject to at the hands of Hindley.

She is enabled to escape by provoking a crisis in the hostility between Heathcliff and Hindley. She deliberately exacerbates the situation, in spite of the danger it involves for Hindley, who dies soon after. And it is a telling circumstance, that in introducing the episode she uses a passive construction to account for Heathcliff's loss of control: '"He was worked up to forget the fiendish prudence he boasted of, and proceeded to murderous violence"' (p. 209). Why does Heathcliff become so excessively violent? Why does he go into a frenzy which is only abated by his own exhaustion? The clue, perhaps, lies in the fact that he was '"worked up"'; immediately prior to his hysterical outburst, he had been in the churchyard, united with the dead body of Cathy. This would have made him realize afresh the pain of separation from her. His violence is thus the violence of extreme frustration, and he vents his terrible anguish at the situation on Hindley whom he sees as a main cause of his having been separated from Cathy during their 'human' lives together. Hindley represents those social forces which had always tried to force him and Cathy apart – which is why he almost tears Hindley apart. Isabella is plainly gratified by the success of her incitements; she says that she is feeling '"the comfort of a quiet conscience within me"' (p. 215) although it is obviously something much baser than that which gives her such a healthy appetite at the same time: '"Nothing hindered me from eating heartily".' As soon as she registers Heathcliff's '"unspeakable sadness"' she finds herself unable to resist '"this chance of sticking in a dart"' (p. 215). Her eagerness to take revenge is expressed in terms that recall the previous torments Heathcliff has undergone – we may remember that at Cathy's death he had howled 'like a savage beast getting goaded to death with knives and spears' (p. 204). Nelly interjects at this stage, and her pious rejoinder makes it clear that she cannot see much difference, morally speaking, between Heathcliff and Isabella. The latter is nevertheless relentless in her desire to '"take an eye for an eye, a tooth for a tooth"' (p. 215) and in this she loses all her moral superiority over her oppressor.

The last words she ever speaks to Heathcliff are to remind him that Cathy chose Edgar rather than him precisely because he has no wealth, no property, and no social status. She uses the very word – '"degrading"' – that Cathy herself had used in justifying her rejection of Heathcliff. It is hardly surprising, therefore, that Heathcliff gives way to a paroxysm of rage. He falls short of actually killing Hindley, but when his old tormentor dies shortly afterwards, it is by no means certain that Heathcliff is not to blame. Joseph is decidedly uneasy about the circumstances of his master's demise:

'Aw'd rayther he'd goan hisseln fur t'doctor! Aw sud uh taen tent uh t'maister better nur him – un he warn't deead when Aw left, nowt uh t' soart!' (p. 222)

Hindley was only twenty-seven at the time of his death and, as Kenneth had earlier announced, he had a very strong constitution, which reduced the likelihood of an early death except by misadventure. It is quite likely (but impossible to prove) that Heathcliff finished him off; in his description of Hindley's last moments, he degrades the sufferer to the level of an animal fit only for the knacker's yard, as if in recognition of the fact that he could go no further than he had already gone in trying to dehumanize him.

Heathcliff may be technically innocent, but in any case the doubt which hangs over his role in the affair raises serious questions about his moral state. Even more disquieting is his attitude as guardian of the newly orphaned Hareton. On the very day of Hindley's funeral, Heathcliff exults in the good fortune which has brought the child into his power:

'Now, my bonny lad, you are *mine*! And we'll see if one tree won't grow as crooked as another, with the same wind to twist it!' (p. 222)

Heathcliff is threatening to use the power of an elemental force to accomplish his design. His threat is reminiscent of the orginal definition of the word 'wuthering', in which the power of nature is measured by comparison with the effects of social deprivation: 'one may guess the power of the north wind, blowing over the edge, by the excessive slant of a few stunted firs at the end of the house; and by a range of gaunt thorns all stretching their limbs one way, as if craving alms of the sun' (p. 46). The pitilessness of the wind can only be expressed in the comparison with a social evil. Heathcliff's metaphor echoes this; it refers to the idea of harnessing a natural force, and directing it to a perverted end. What this reveals to us is his own moral state. His offences against Hareton, and the other members of the younger generation, are simply the most perverted and unforgivable of his acts of aggression.

Not content with brutalizing the son of the man who brutalized him, he boasts of having acquired the youth's fondness for him as well. He develops a considerable attachment to Hareton in return, but encourages him to fall in love with the younger Catherine precisely so that he can be cheated out of her. In other words, he wants to wreck the life of someone he had come to care for merely to satisfy the logic of vengeance. None the less, at the same time as he plots further degradation for Hareton, he cannot help referring to him as 'him' whereas his own son Linton is instantly degraded to 'it' from the moment of his arrival. This is the same style in which he himself had been greeted on his first arrival at the Heights, when even Nelly had referred to him as 'it'. Heathcliff goes even further in making Linton unwelcome: he confronts this product of gentility with vernacular forms of speech, and pulls the child around to examine him as if he were a piece of livestock.

He frankly admits that the only reason he is able to endure the presence of Isabella's son at the Heights is so as to be able to complete his revenge by installing Linton as lord of the Grange estates. What is more ominous, he has already considered the possibility that in the event of Linton's death, all the property would be transferred to him. He is quite open about this, and even predicts when his son is likely to die in the latter's hearing. Linton comes to fear his father so much that even when Heathcliff is absent his menacing power is constantly felt; when forced to attend a meeting with Catherine, Linton transfers all his father's most frightening qualities on to the landscape, as if there were no escape from them:

'I thought I heard my father,' he gasped, glancing up to the frowning nab above us. 'You are sure nobody spoke?' (p. 295)

Heathcliff manages to entrap Catherine by dictating Linton's love letters to her, and by forcing her to break her father's quarantine with the news that Linton is dying for love of her. Once she is duped into returning to the Heights, Heathcliff blocks off her escape and uses physical constraint to ensure her marriage to Linton. The violence of his coercions leads Nelly to resort to the 'diabolical' vocabulary, but already his ferocity is beginning to seem willed, and even mannered:

'Had I been born where laws are less strict, and tastes less dainty, I should treat myself to a slow vivisection of those two as an evening's amusement'. (p. 302)

It is really no more than a hideous reflex action which makes him go on teasing his prisoner: '"Miss Linton, I shall enjoy myself remarkably in thinking your father will be miserable; I shall not sleep for satisfaction"' (p. 306). But when Catherine reacts to this treatment, not with fear and hatred, but with understanding and kindness, Heathcliff is evidently distressed by her similarity to his own Cathy. He is stirred to verbal brutality as a self-defensive manoeuvre, but at the same time he shakes with emotion, and cannot even look into the girl's eyes. He is at his wildest when most sharply reminded of his greatest loss, as when he struggles with Catherine over the portrait of Cathy, and strikes her so hard that her cheek is '"cut on the inside, against her teeth"' (p. 313).

After her temporary escape to the Grange, in time to witness her father's death, Heathcliff turns up to recapture her; his approach is heralded by a servant's warning that '"that devil Heathcliff"' was coming through the court' (p. 317) – his devilishness is now taken as a matter of course. On the death of Linton, he badgers Catherine with the need to know exactly what she is feeling; this is part of the purpose of his experiment – to see if he can provoke in others the kind of feelings he had at being separated from Cathy.

In spite of everything, Heathcliff still has weak spots, even traces of tenderness. It is in fact his capacity for feeling that is gradually killing him. And as he gets closer to death, he suffers increasingly from the likeness to Cathy he can see in the faces of both Hareton and Catherine. The tables are turned to the extent that he begins to address the latter as a '"fiend"' with '"infernal eyes"', and the spectacle of the two young people together reminds him of himself and Cathy at the most, or rather the only, idyllic stage of their lives. Finally, he loses the '"faculty of enjoying their destruction"' (p. 353).

Nelly's final assessment of him involves a typical compound of superstition and common sense. She revolves the idea that he might be a 'ghoul, or a vampire', and remembers having read about such 'hideous, incarnate demons' (p. 359). On the other hand, she admits that it is 'absurd nonsense' (p. 360) to think of Heathcliff as devilish, once you know the truth about the formation of his character, as she does. She is, quite simply, in two minds about him; and her dream, in which she is faced with the task of dictating an inscription for his gravestone, and can think of nothing to say except 'Heathcliff', seems much more adequate in its refusal to try and fit him into existing categories and to ignore his uniqueness.

Heathcliff's last words to Nelly (which are his last words to any living being) demonstrate that the idea of his 'devilishness' is a matter of wry humour to him: '"I believe you think me a fiend!" he said, with his dismal laugh, "something too horrible to live under a decent roof!"' (p. 364). From this, it would seem that his fiendishness is something deliberately assumed rather than inherent in his nature. Nevertheless, when Nelly discovers his dead body, Joseph is at hand to provide an orthodox assurance of his evil. Joseph's influence on the way that others view Heathcliff cannot be underestimated, as the 'diabolic' vocabulary is thick in the air with him around. His rather obtuse loyalty to Hindley, through thick and thin, shows that his judgement of character bears a rather strained relationship to the conventional morality he dins into the ears of anyone who will listen. His attempts to foster hatred between Hareton and Heathcliff confirm that his Christianity is in the letter rather than in the spirit.

The accusations of 'devilishness' must be taken as a register of feeling rather than as a reliable means of identifying the moral state of a character. Heathcliff's own accusations – which seem justifiable at the time – of Cathy as being a '"devil"', and of Edgar as being a '"fiend"', ought to give us due warning of that. In conclusion, what makes Heathcliff so unacceptable to the majority of the other characters is that his behaviour is so inexplicable to them; he does not fit into any pattern that they recognize. The position that he occupies, between different states, is summed up by Frank Kermode in his study of the novel:

Heathcliff is then as it were between names, as between families (he is the door through which Earnshaw passes into Linton, and out again to Earnshaw). He is often introduced, as if characteristically, standing outside, or entering, or leaving, a door. He is in and out of the Earnshaw family simultaneously; servant and child of the family (like Hareton, whom he puts in the same position, he helps to indicate the archaic nature of the house's society, the lack of sharp social division, which is not characteristic of the Grange). His origins are equally betwixt and between: the gutter or the royal origin imagined for him by Nelly; prince or pauper, American or Lascar, child of God or devil. This betweenness persists, I think: Heathcliff, for instance, fluctuates between poverty and riches; also between virility and impotence. To Catherine he is between brother and lover; he slept with her as a child, and again in death, but not between latency and extinction. He has much force, yet fathers an exceptionally puny child. Domestic yet savage like the dogs, bleak yet full of fire like the house, he bestrides the great opposites: love and death (the necrophiliac confession), culture and nature ('half-civilized ferocity') in a posture that certainly cannot be explained by any generic formula ('Byronic' or 'Gothic').

He stands also between a past and a future; when his force expires the old Earnshaw family moves into the future associated with the civilized Grange, where the insane authoritarianism of the Heights is a thing of the past, where there are cultivated distinctions between gentle and simple – a new world in the more civil south.[28]

Kermode is making out a case for Heathcliff as the 'principal instrument of mediation' between the generic opposites with which the novel abounds. It is time to explore the much more fundamental mediation of the narrators, whose own strengths and limitations must be probed as deeply as those of Cathy and Heathcliff themselves.

8. Narrators

One of the most striking aspects of *Wuthering Heights* is its proliferation of narrators. None of these narrators can be identified with the voice of the author herself, and each one is prevented by class, education and personality from a full understanding of the protagonists, Cathy and Heathcliff. On the one hand, this gives us, the readers, an important role to play in deciding what to accept and what to reject of the accounts at our disposal. On the other hand, it is likely to produce a radical uncertainty about the central meaning of the experience that all the narrators are trying to make sense of. It is of crucial importance that the text encourages us to dissent from the viewpoints of Lockwood and Nelly, the two main narrators. It means that we are likely to depreciate the value of gentility and common sense, no matter what we decide to think about the lovers. It is equally important that Cathy and Heathcliff are given only short passages of narration, because if their story were presented mostly from their own point of view, it would diminish the force produced by its collision with orthodox modes of thought. The imaginative authority of their experience is made possible by its impact on narrators who regard it as an enigma.

The number of narrators is actually seven. Of these, neither Zillah nor the younger Catherine is given enough space to seriously affect our understanding of events. We have already considered the episodes covered by Cathy's diary and Isabella's two reports; we have also referred to Heathcliff's accounts of the visit to Thrushcross Grange, and the night he spends at Cathy's grave. What remains is to check for any developments in the frame-narrative of Lockwood, and to assess the full extent of Nelly's control over what we know of the events, not to mention her control over the events themselves.

The first thing to be said about Lockwood is how little this extraordinary tale of passion seems to affect him. He shows a dilettante's appreciation of a good story but no real involvement in the lives of the characters, whom he says he is interested in '"more or less"' (p. 102). As a matter of fact, he *loses* interest in them for a considerable period of time, and is only roused to hear the rest of the story out of sheer boredom:

Why not have up Mrs Dean to finish her tale? I can recollect its chief incidents, as far as she had gone. Yes, I remember her hero had run off, and never been heard of for three years: and the heroine was married: I'll ring; she'll be delighted to find me capable of talking cheerfully. (p. 130)

He reacts to Nelly's narrative precisely as to a fiction; his use of the novelistic terms 'hero' and 'heroine' suggest that it is as alien to him, as unconnected with his own life, as a fantastic romance would be. *As* a romance, however, it is sufficiently to his taste, and he even admits that Nelly is 'on the whole, a very fair narrator, and I don't think I could improve her style' (p. 192). The fact that Nelly has managed to frame her account in terms agreeable to Lockwood will hardly reassure the critical reader. In spite of Lockwood's apparent detachment, it is Nelly's intention to use her skill not only to draw him into the story, but into the lives of the characters as well:

'These things happened last winter, sir,' said Mrs Dean; 'hardly more than a year ago. Last winter, I did not think, at another twelve months' end, I should be amusing a stranger to the family with relating them! Yet, who knows how long you'll be a stranger? You're too young to rest always contented, living by yourself; and I some way fancy, no one could see Catherine Linton, and not love her. You smile; but why do you look so lively and interested when I talk about her? and why have you asked me to hang her picture over your fireplace? and why –'

'Stop, my good friend!' I cried. 'It may be very possible that *I* should love her; but would she love me? I doubt it too much to venture my tranquillity, by running into temptation; and then my home is not here. I'm of the busy world, and to its arms I must return. Go on. Was Catherine obedient to her father's commands?' (p. 288)

Nelly appears, here, virtually as a pander. Her desire to cajole Lockwood into a romantic attachment to Catherine is typical of her tendency to interfere in the lives of others, particularly when she has something to gain by it. The crassness of her overture is matched by Lockwood's clumsy insincerity in completely belying his assumption of a hermit's character. He constantly toys with the idea of a flirtation with Catherine, but loses all his self-possession when faced with the possibility of a real involvement. His timidity is not confined to his dealings with the opposite sex; he is equally chary in the field of general ideas:

Do you believe such people *are* happy in the other world, sir? I'd give a great deal to know.

I declined answering Mrs Dean's question, which struck me as something heterodox. (p. 202)

When Lockwood resumes the role of main narrator towards the end of the novel, it is to record his impressions of yet another visit to the Heights. He now knows as much as any outsider could know about the private lives of its inhabitants, and yet he makes no greater allowance for the oddity of their behaviour than he did when he knew nothing whatever about them. He still sees only Hareton's lack of grace, rather than his humanity; indeed, his sense of superiority seems to have been bolstered rather than shaken by the revelation of what it means to have an emotional life: 'Living among clowns and misanthropists, she probably cannot appreciate a better class of people, when she meets them' (p. 335).

Most absurd of all, perhaps, is the fact that he still expects to be treated with the common forms of politeness. And his alarm at the prospect of social embarrassment is so highly developed that he has to take special care to remove any suspicion that the letter from Nelly which he hands to Catherine might actually be from him. Heathcliff establishes the fatuousness of Lockwood's self-image projected at the start of the book by mocking his lack of stamina in '"being banished from the world"' (p. 334). But the real liability of having Lockwood as a narrator is less obvious, and less easy to efface; he may be innocuous in his own person, but this does not detract from the insidiousness of his language:

The little wretch had done her utmost to hurt her cousin's sensitive though uncultivated feelings, and a physical argument was the only mode he had of balancing the account, and repaying its effects on the inflicter. (p. 333)

What this nonchalant account of a domestic upset reveals is Lockwood's readiness to explain the working of emotions in the light of a metaphor of exchange, in which feeling is subordinated to a trading of advantages; moreover, this emotional transaction is conducted in the spirit of an eye-for-an-eye vindictiveness. In other words, Lockwood is once more disclosing his similarity to Heathcliff, with the vital difference that Heathcliff is open in admitting to the perversity of his motivation, whereas Lockwood seeks to disguise the truth in his own case by shifting everything into the realm of metaphor. And this, in a sense, is what civility is all about.

Lockwood's inability to learn anything from the story amounts to a *refusal* to learn. The unnecessary degree of stress he lays on his own difference from those who are caught up in the events is partly an over-conscientious attempt to stop himself thinking about the similarities. The precautions he takes to have us believe that he is immune to any foreign influences from the Heights are too elaborate. On his return to the Grange after an absence of only a few months, his professed inability to remember even the name of the local village, Gimmerton, is scarcely credible: 'my residence in that locality had already grown dim and dreamy' (p. 336). And although we already know the frivolousness of his temperament, his repeated insistence on the aimlessness of his journey back to the area is enough to make us wonder whether the opposite is not true. The moment he is made aware of a change in the mutual regard of Catherine and Hareton, his dilatoriness vanishes, and he admits to 'being moved thereto by a mingled sense of curiosity, and envy that grew as I lingered . . . I bit my lip, in spite, at having thrown away the chance I might have had, of doing something besides staring at its smiting beauty' (p. 338). In the last clause, which refers to Catherine's face, he bursts out with a much more physical verb than he has previously allowed himself to use in describing the attractiveness of a woman. Lockwood has more at stake than he owns up to in trying to keep his distance, both physically and linguistically, from the genuine commitments and betrayals at the Heights.

There is a sense in which Nelly's role in the novel involves one long betrayal of trust. Certainly, the reader would be wrong to place too much confidence in the reputation she has derived from Charlotte Brontë's 1850 *Preface* to the novel, in which she is described as 'a specimen of true benevolence and homely fidelity' (p. 39). Nelly is often weaned away from her homely fidelity in pursuit of the main chance, and the methods she employs on the way earn her the title of '"hidden enemy"' (p. 166); she is very choosy about whom she wishes well to. When we are first trying to get the measure of her in the early chapters, she almost finds it unnecessary to indicate which social group she belongs to: '"Miss Cathy is of us – I mean, of the Lintons"' (p. 75). This tendency to identify with the gentry has always been unhesitating. Her accommodating attitude towards Lockwood is enough to demonstrate how much she loves to hobnob with the 'quality'. From the moment of Cathy's first return from Thrushcross Grange, Nelly had shown a certain admiration for the change it had wrought in her. She soon warmed to her new role of 'playing lady's maid' (p. 95) and, once the first excitement had died down, addressed herself to 'the speckless purity of my particular care – the scoured and well-swept floor' (p. 95). Her predisposition for gentility seems confirmed by the mood in which she gives 'due inward applause' to this accomplished piece of housekeeping. Not long afterwards, when she encourages Heathcliff to frame high notions of his birth, she is obviously trying to project on to him the inspiration she derives from her own daydreams of advancement.

When the dearly wished-for move from the Heights to the Grange occurs, Nelly soon begins to stand on her dignity. Time and again she shows her conscious superiority over the other domestics. She is much more abrupt, savage even, with her fellow servants than her employers are:

'Oh, dear, dear! What mun we have next? Master, master, our young lady –'
  'Hold your noise!' cried I hastily, enraged at her clamorous manner.
  'Speak lower, Mary – What is the matter?' said Mr Linton. 'What ails your young lady?' (p. 169)

When she returns to Wuthering Heights on a visit – in search of the truant younger Catherine – she behaves with an obnoxious haughtiness towards the 'woman whom I knew' (p. 223) who has succeeded her as housekeeper. Nelly's sense of her own worthiness is such that she never misses a chance of stressing it, even at the cost of being insensitive towards others. When she follows Isabella to the Heights, in the hope of bringing her back to the Grange, she is taken aback by the shameful condition of the place:

There never was such a dreary, dismal scene as the formerly cheerful house presented! I must confess that, if I had been in the young lady's place, I would, at least, have swept the hearth, and wiped the tables with a duster. (p. 183)

Nelly has now 'developed' socially to the extent that she is shocked by Isabella's not being prepared to keep up appearances. There is an ugly hint of complacency ('I must confess that . . . I would, at least . . .') in her deprecation, which makes her almost as bad as Lockwood, with his fetish for presentability. What she is not pausing to consider is the degree of suffering that would have led up to this; and she has no excuse, because this is *after* she has read Isabella's distracted letter.

Nelly sometimes shows a keener interest in the property of the Lintons than the Lintons do themselves, as on the death of Hindley, when she persuades Edgar to let her visit the Heights, partly because Hindley has been left in a 'friendless condition', and partly because Edgar 'ought to and must inquire how the property was left, and look over the concerns of his brother-in-law' (p. 221). She frequently oversteps her responsibilities as a servant, as when she decides what to hide and what to reveal to Edgar about Catherine's relationship with Linton. Edgar is unaware of the viciousness of Linton's nature, but Nelly refrains from correcting his error, through what she calls 'pardonable weakness' (p. 297). It is a moot point whether it is pardonable or not, when so much of her life is spent in weighing up the relative advantages of hiding and revealing.

The very language with which she relates the story is a language of compromise – it is her chief means of dissassociating herself from the world of the Heights. As Lockwood says to her, '"Excepting a few provincialisms of slight consequence, you have no marks of the manners which I am habituated to consider as peculiar to your class"' (p. 103), and Nelly laughs with pleasure at this remark, flattered that Lockwood should find enough cause to welcome her as a member of the same linguistic community as himself. However, she goes on to congratulate herself for her reasonableness, and attributes this to two things:

> 'I have undergone sharp discipline which has taught me wisdom; and then, I have read more than you would fancy, Mr Lockwood. You could not open a book in this library that I have not looked into, and got something out of also; unless it be that range of Greek and Latin, and that of French – and those I know one from another, it is as much as you can expect of a poor man's daughter.' (p. 103)

Nelly's belief that she has derived wisdom from 'sharp discipline' practically disqualifies her from being able to sympathize with Heathcliff, whose own experience of sharp discipline has led him to what she regards as virtual insanity; besides which, her evident approval of the principle of subordination must prejudice her against the nonconformism of Cathy and Heathcliff. The rest of what she says conflates the wisdom which comes from experience with the wisdom which comes from books. And this deference to precept is also potentially obstructive to the understanding of what has every appearance of being an unprecedented situation.

As a matter of fact, Nelly's response to any eventuality is to encapsulate it in the appropriate 'sentence'. She is always extremely prompt with her conventional wisdom, and her speech is often proverbial in form even when she is not directly uttering a proverb. She is an inveterate moralizer: often a glib one, and just as often a tactless one, as her tart remarks to Cathy and Heathcliff show, when the one is at a critical stage of her illness, and the other is at death's door. What chiefly grates with the reader is the smugness with which Nelly endorses her maxims; when she patronizes her own employer with the reassurance that '"people who do their duty are always finally rewarded"' (p. 289) it begs the question of how often she does her own duty, either towards those she is contracted to serve, or towards those who have a right to expect her help on the grounds of common humanity.

One of Nelly's most pronounced characteristics is her pragmatism. She does not scruple to abandon those who have outlived their usefulness. After tacitly admitting that Cathy is necessary to her as a means of access to Thrushcross Grange (she says 'I got Miss Catherine and myself to Thrushcross Grange' as if it were a project of her own conception) she promptly ceases to further Cathy's interests where these are at variance with her own. As she puts it: 'My heart invariably cleaved to the master's, in preference to Catherine's side' (p. 146). When she fails to negotiate the retention of Linton Heathcliff at the Grange she delivers him up to his father, and soon finds a suitable pretext for washing her hands of him altogether: 'I divined . . . that utter lack of sympathy had rendered young Heathcliff selfish and disagreeable . . . and my interest in him, consequently, decayed' (p. 246). Her divination is effected, not by experience, but by report.

More striking is the series of changes in her attitude towards Hareton. While still at Wuthering Heights, she says that he was more than all the world to her, although this does not stop her from losing all interest in him for several years. By the end of the book, she is declaring that '"The crown of all my wishes will be the union"' (p. 346) of Catherine and Hareton, although nothing had been further from her thoughts a short while before, when she had tried to act as marriage-broker to Lockwood. The only inducement for her to switch from opposition to acceptance of the idea of Catherine's union with Hareton is that Hareton has become a landowner in the interim.

Nelly is at her most brutally selfish during the last moments that Cathy and Heathcliff have together. In her anxiety lest Edgar should walk in on the two lovers, she describes as the '"most diabolical deed"' that Heathcliff has ever done, his placing her own situation in jeopardy: '"We are all done for – master, mistress, and servant"' (p. 199). When Cathy falls unconscious, she is 'sincerely glad' to observe the fact: '"She's fainted or dead," I thought; "so much the better"' (p. 199). It is surely an unpardonable degree of pragmatism that can greet the death of another because it is convenient to oneself.

But how has Heathcliff managed to secure this interview with Cathy? And how is it that Nelly remains to witness the incredibly intimate scene? The answer has to do with Nelly's irresistible need to manipulate the course of relationships whose intimacy she is inevitably excluded from. She is fundamentally unable to mind her own business, and often shows a deep satisfaction at being 'in the know'. She also shows a curious avidity for crisis in the relationships of others, and it may be that she is unable to prevent herself from provoking such crises. How else are we to explain her behaviour towards the younger Catherine when the latter is found to be exchanging love letters with Linton? Nelly has all the evidence of such a correspondence long before she does anything about it, so why does she not stop it sooner? It may be that she allows it to grow, the better to satisfy her incurable need to spy on the intimacy of others.

After a due period of time has elapsed, she empties the letters from their hiding-place and takes them 'to examine at leisure in my own chamber' (p. 258). From what she says of their contents, it is clearly an absorbing task for her, yet she claims to have turned over only 'as many as I thought proper' (p. 259), which is somewhat ironic, since she has already gone beyond the bounds of propriety (at no stage does she see fit to inform the parent of the girl concerned). She is now in a position to confront Catherine with the evidence of her misdemeanour; but instead of doing this, she takes an uncalled-for step involving even greater furtiveness. She intercepts one of the letters that Catherine has written to Linton; this is completely unnecessary, and is only done to satisfy her own curiosity. When Catherine tries to excuse her own conduct by claiming that she is in love with Linton, Nelly is justifiably unwilling to believe that what she feels is really love. However, the amount of scorn and derision that Nelly employs is out of all proportion in the context, and we may question her authority as an arbiter of what is or isn't love when she has never been in love in her life. Neither has she experienced sexual intimacy (Joseph makes no bones about the fact that she is physically unattractive). As a young girl she may have had an unusually close attachment to her foster-brother, Hindley, but that is all. Denied the intensity of passion in her own life, Nelly is simultaneously sceptical about, and parasitical upon, the presence of passion in others.

Nelly's jealous curiosity, her desire to get inside the relationships of other people, and the air of moral aloofness she preserves at the same time, often make her handling of other people's problems disastrous. It is a disaster when she fails to disclose the hidden presence of Heathcliff during the first part of Cathy's confession of the nature of her feelings for him and Edgar. When Heathcliff gets up to leave, Nelly starts, and bids Cathy to hush:

'Why?' she asked, gazing nervously round.

'Joseph is here,' I answered, catching, opportunely, the roll of his cartwheels up the road . . . (p. 121)

She tells an outright lie, when the truth might have sent Cathy after Heathcliff in time to prevent misunderstanding and avert disaster. When Cathy goes on to explain the depth of her feelings for Heathcliff, Nelly loses patience with her:

'If I can make any sense of your nonsense, Miss,' I said, 'it only goes to convince me that you are ignorant of the duties you undertake in marrying; or else, that you are a wicked, unprincipled girl. But trouble me with no more secrets. I'll not promise to keep them.' (p. 122)

Nelly identifies two failings in Cathy: the first, an ignorance of the duties of marriage, is a shortcoming she could do something about, but doesn't; the second, the idea that Cathy is wicked and unprincipled, shows a complete inability to grasp the nature of the problem. She stresses the value of her own 'sense' over Cathy's 'nonsense' because of her vested interest in propriety, her need to maintain a sense of her own superiority, and her nervous rejection of a part of life which intrigues her but which she has had no share in. There is little room for self-doubt in Nelly's reflections on the episode, although her dogged reinforcement of the statement that Cathy is solely to blame for everything should be called to account.

Nelly's most damaging resort to falsehood occurs during the onset of Cathy's illness. After Heathcliff's return, Cathy intends to use emotional blackmail to force Edgar to let her keep him as a friend. Nelly's common sense tells her that anyone capable of switching on their fits of passion is equally capable of switching them off again, but she cannot appreciate the intensity of Cathy's distress. She regards as mere tantrums what the reader can perceive as the signs of an unbearable conflict in Cathy's nature. When the interview between husband and wife concludes with a paroxysm on Cathy's part, Nelly (who has overheard everything, she is such an incorrigible eavesdropper) makes the breathtaking announcement that '"There is nothing in the world the matter"' (p. 157) even though 'in her own heart' she realizes the crude inadequacy of such a no-nonsense approach. Any slight misgivings she may have vanish in a matter of days, and she is soon ready to take pride in the fact that she is the 'one sensible soul' (p. 158) at the Grange. She completely misjudges the seriousness of Cathy's attempt to starve herself, which makes her in large measure responsible for the extent of Cathy's physical deterioration. She never informs Edgar of the extremity of the case until it is far too late.

When Cathy demands to know how Edgar is reacting to his wife's decline, Nelly lies: she convinces Cathy that Edgar is indifferent to her fate. Cathy puts her on her honour: '"Are you speaking the truth about him now? Take care"' (p. 159), but this does not prevent Nelly from creating the impression that Edgar is more interested in the condition of his library than in the condition of his wife, even though she herself has told the reader that he has '"never opened"' any books during all this time. Cathy's condition worsens as a direct result of this: '"She could not bear the notion which I had put into her head of Mr Linton's philosophical resignation"' (p. 160), and she comes to regard Nelly increasingly as a sinister figure, although the latter puts this down to insanity. In spite of the state which Cathy gets into, Nelly herself is taken off guard by the greatness of Edgar's shock on discovering the gravity of his wife's illness. She makes a craven attempt to defend her own conduct:

> He was silent; the haggardness of Mrs Linton's appearance smote him speechless, and he could only glance from her to me in horrified astonishment.
>
> 'She's been fretting here,' I continued, 'and eating scarcely anything, and never complaining, and she would admit none of us till this evening, and so we couldn't inform you of her state, as we were not aware of it ourselves, but it is nothing.'
>
> I felt I uttered my explanations awkwardly; the master frowned. (p. 165)

In her anxiety to excuse herself, Nelly tries to extend the blame to others (she uses the first person plural although nobody else has been involved). Her repetition of the diagnosis 'it is nothing' sounds particularly lame, in view of the dramatic change that Cathy has undergone. Nelly evidently feels her own culpability. But this is only for a moment; as soon as Edgar starts to reprimand her, she swiftly regains her composure and does not see why she should accept the least degree of guilt: '"I began to defend myself, thinking it too bad to be blamed for another's wicked waywardness!"' (p. 166).

In the midst of this crisis, she makes the discovery that Isabella has eloped with Heathcliff, but withholds the information, on her own responsibility, even though there is '"a bare possibility of overtaking them if pursued instantly"' (p. 168). In her subsequent visit to the Heights, she agrees to assist Heathcliff in making contact with Cathy, although the reasons she gives for doing this can hardly be said to pass muster. To start with, she exaggerates the degree of opposition she had mounted against the idea – '"Well, Mr Lockwood, I argued and complained, and flatly refused him fifty times"' – which only serves to accentuate her final capitulation: '"but in the long run he forced me to an agreement"' (p. 190). She effectively draws a veil over this decision by emphasizing her own passivity and by having recourse to a curiously insubstantial pretext: '"I thought I prevented another explosion by my compliance; and I thought, too, it might create a favourable crisis in Catherine's mental illness"' (p. 190). The probability that Nelly herself does not believe in this as a justification is increased by the fact that she forgets all about it; by the time that she comes to deliver Heathcliff's letter to Cathy, she is in a state of mind in which '"I could not guess how its receipt would affect Catherine"' (p. 192). She concludes by virtually admitting the weakness of the ground she is standing on when she promises '"that that betrayal of trust, if it merited so harsh an appellation, should be the last"' (pp. 190–91). There is special pleading here which underlines the flimsiness of her excuse; but even so, the attempt to save face might have some small force if the promise were kept, which it is not.

Later on, she encourages the younger Catherine to deceive her own father about the number and nature of her visits to the Heights, and she is cruelly deceptive towards Linton. She lulls him into the expectation that Heathcliff will be a loving father, '"fonder of you than any uncle"' (p. 241), and that the Heights will be an agreeable place to live. Linton's unpleasantness makes him a character difficult to sympathize with at the best of times, but it is none the less pathetic and unjust that he should be brought to give the benefit of the doubt to persons and conditions that will prove intolerable to him.

Nelly's role in the development of Catherine's and Linton's intimacy is one of endless temporizing and backsliding. She reaches the stage where she has betrayed confidences so often that she can do it without a second thought, 'walking straight from her room to his, and relating the whole story, with the exception of her conversations with her cousin, and any mention of Hareton' (p. 286). She always edits the facts to suit herself – she becomes a past master in knowing what to conceal and what to reveal: 'As soon as he recovered, I related our compulsory visit, and detention at the Heights: I said Heathcliff forced me to go in, which was not quite true' (p. 314).

She is still covering her tracks at the time of Heathcliff's death, when she conceals 'the fact of his having swallowed nothing for four days, fearing it might lead to trouble' (p. 365); the trouble she anticipates is left rather vague – perhaps she has an uncomfortable feeling that the manner of his death would reflect badly on her.

If it is not already clear why we should hesitate before accepting Nelly as an impartial judge of Heathcliff's character, we should be alerted by the fact that it is Heathcliff who is the shrewdest judge of *her* character. He makes specific reference to her 'prying' on two separate occasions and offers a blunt objection to her '"double dealing"'. On one occasion, Nelly bridles at the insinuation that she is not minding her own business:

'I'm not putting the question through idle curiosity, but –'
'You are putting the question through very idle curiosity,' he interrupted, with a laugh. (p. 358)

Heathcliff's laugh is the laugh of recognition – once more Nelly has given way to her insatiable need to meddle. All this can only add to the antagonism of a woman whose commitment to Heathcliff's oldest enemy has never died out; she is probably unaware of the strength of her attachment to Hindley until the moment of the latter's death:

I confess this blow was greater to me than the shock of Mrs Linton's death: ancient associations lingered round my heart; I sat down in the porch, and wept as for a blood relation, desiring Kenneth to get another servant to introduce him to the master. (p. 220)

Her compassion, which is one of Nelly's positive qualities, might seem to make her a more trustworthy narrator than Lockwood, but it also shows how she might be biased against Heathcliff, in spite of her resistance to Isabella's wild assertions about him.

Only once does Nelly begin to offer a criticism of her own behaviour along the lines we have been pursuing here:

I seated myself in a chair, and rocked, to and fro, passing harsh judgment on my many derelictions of duty; from which, it struck me then, all the misfortunes of all my employers sprang. It was not the case, in reality, I am aware; but it was, in my imagination, that dismal night, and I thought Heathcliff himself less guilty than I. (p. 308)

Nelly exaggerates; and we should not exploit either her candour or her attempt to over-compensate for her misgivings. But it does not require too much ingenuity to argue that the accusations which she brings against herself (and then withdraws) are at least partly true. It is so typical of Nelly that this moment of self-awareness reverts to self-delusion. It is, precisely, a *moment* of insight which she subsequently retracts, a passing mood immediately thought better of. The fact that she sits down to do her thinking in a rocking-chair, whose very motion gives an infantile kind of comfort, suggests that she only starts this train of thought in order to exonerate herself and set her mind at rest.

Nelly is the most stable and level-headed character in the novel; but her common sense is just as often a limitation as it is a positive asset. Her profound urge to conform often compromises her behaviour towards those who are less in sympathy with the conventions than she is. She is prepared to lie and even betray as a means of thwarting any disruption of her adopted system of values. Her ambitiousness leads her to a more active role than she is strictly entitled to, and her officiousness is often greater than that of her 'magisterial' employers (even her surname *Dean* is authoritarian- and institutional-sounding). The language of gentility which she has so carefully acquired earns her her place in society by excluding the transgressions of Cathy and Heathcliff from its meanings. Her desire to supervise the affairs of others is only harmonized with her pursuit of the legitimate and the decorous in the outcome of the developing love between Hareton and Catherine. When this is sanctioned by their marriage and removal to Thrushcross Grange, the issues of the story are at last within Nelly's imaginative range as narrator.*

---

* Emily Brontë's attitude to Nelly is evidently a strained one. Edward Chitham suggests that 'Nelly is Ellen and is obviously related to Ellis (Emily's pseudonym), and her Christian name. Like many of the parts conned by this actress, Nelly is a part of Emily, the well-read housekeeper at Haworth parsonage.'[29]

9. The Second Generation

The latter part of the novel, which deals with the second generation comprising the younger Catherine, Hareton and Linton, is in a sense a revision, a re-casting of the issues of the first part. To be more precise, it is a kind of reversal of the movement of the first part, or an unfolding of its complexities, as Frank Kermode suggests when he draws attention to the order of the scribbled names discovered by Lockwood: '*Catherine Earnshaw, Catherine Heathcliff, Catherine Linton*. Read from left to right they recapitulate Catherine Earnshaw's story; read from right to left, the story of her daughter, Catherine Linton.'[30] In the terms agreed by the characters who survive, the book ends on a positive note; but what exactly are the gains made by the younger Catherine in her reversal of the pattern of her mother's life? What is it that enables her and Hareton to survive and prosper, whose absence had led to apparent failure in the lives of Cathy and Heathcliff? Conversely, does the second generation lose anything worth keeping of the quality of experience in the first part?

The second part of the novel commences on a note of blending and selection, where the first part had swung repeatedly between irreconcilable extremes. We are told that the younger Catherine is a combination of Earnshaw and Linton traits: a combination, moreover, of the positive qualities of both parents – which means that any faults she has will be due to her social circumstances. Her social circumstances are centred on the possessiveness of her father: 'He took her education entirely on himself' (p. 224). What the narrowness of his influence entails is a bullying attitude to servants that will affect the character of her first few meetings with Hareton. She is socially insulated to such a degree that, until she reaches the age of thirteen, she has never been beyond the grounds of Thrushcross Grange by herself. As Nelly remarks, without any trace of censure, 'she was a perfect recluse' (p. 225). It only needs the reader to ask why she has to be such a perfect recluse to provoke the reflection that Edgar is being just as selfish, in his own way, in the control of a young person's life, as Heathcliff is to prove in respect of Linton.

It is also worth bearing in mind the magnitude of effort required to throw off such deeply rooted influences. There are in fact strong hints already that underneath all this narrowly directed 'culture' is the beginning of a longing for the same things that excited the interest of Cathy as a young girl:

'Ellen, how long will it be before I can walk to the top of these hills? I wonder what lies on the other side – is it the sea?'

'No, Miss Cathy,' I would answer, 'it is hills again just like these.' (p. 225)

When Catherine shows a particular interest in the golden rocks of Penistone Crags, Nelly's attempt to discourage her interest only serves to enhance it:

'Oh, you have been on them!' she cried, gleefully. 'Then I can go, too, when I am a woman . . .' (p. 225)

The sexual connotation of Catherine's hope that she will reach Penistone Crags when she is an adult woman is neither idle nor accidental; Penistone is a real place in the West Riding with a quarry whose tunnelled grit face corresponds to the 'Fairy cave' which Catherine wants to visit. According to local tradition, anyone going into the tunnel would marry within the year.[31] These circumstances alone are enough to make Catherine's impatience with the civilized bounds of Thrushcross Grange seem prophetic of the way in which she is to outreach them. The fact that it is Hareton who opens 'the mysteries of the Fairy cave' (p. 233) to her right at the start of their relationship means that her restlessness has already found what it needs, although this is beyond her present realization.

It is ironic that Catherine's first adventure is to break out of the bounds of Thrushcross Grange, because her mother's first adventure had been to break *into* the same bounds. Catherine starts off on her escapade with her mind in the realms of fancy: 'Catherine came to me, one morning, at eight o'clock, and said she was that day an Arabian merchant, going to cross the desert with his caravan' (p. 227). This fairy-tale aura is precisely what Cathy had assumed on her first visit to the Grange, after the Lintons had taken her in; it is precisely what is shattered at the Heights. Its lingering around the Grange suggests that the Lintons exist in a world of illusions.

When Catherine arrives at the Heights, her experience is partly a repetition of Lockwood's and Isabella's (from this point on, the second generation is shown as being constantly in danger of falling into the same traps as the first). Hareton and Catherine show a mutual astonishment at each other's language – the result of their both being recluses. At this stage, Catherine appears to share in full measure the damaging limitations of her class, assuming that Hareton's inability to understand her is proof of his subservient state. Hareton, in turn, is far from untouched by his environment, and actually sounds like a replica of Joseph:

'I'll see thee damned, before I be *thy* servant!' growled the lad.
  'You'll see me *what*?' asked Catherine in surprise.
  'Damned – thou saucy witch!' he replied. (p. 230)

Since the language that Catherine understands best is the language of deference and tribute, it is hardly surprising that the expressions Hareton 'had held to her rankled in her heart; she who was always "love," and "darling," and "queen," and "angel," with everybody at the Grange, to be insulted so shockingly by a stranger!' (p. 233). But in spite of his roughness, Hareton shows himself capable of sympathizing with Catherine's distress, and he makes more concessions than she does. He tries to propitiate her anger with the gift of 'a fine crooked-legged terrier whelp from the kennel' (p. 231) but his peace-offering is rejected. His fundamental decency is recognized by Nelly, whose description of his character turns on a metaphorical distinction between 'nature' and 'culture'. The best things in Hareton are rooted in naturalness, but stand in need of cultivation if they are to flourish:

Good things lost amid a wilderness of weeds, to be sure, whose rankness far over-topped their neglected growth; yet notwithstanding, evidence of a wealthy soil that might yield luxuriant crops, under other and favourable circumstances. (p. 231)

The focus of Hareton's cultivation is his emergence from illiteracy, and in this the key role goes to Catherine. The full significance of his gaining control of language appears in the moment that she discovers he cannot read, when she asks the meaning of the inscription over the door. Once Hareton has acquired the culture that enables him to read the inscription – which tells him of his birthright – he is ready to take his place in society.

Linton is the most unnatural character in the book, which may seem a little odd, considering he is the son of Heathcliff. The point is, he is not so much the son of Heathcliff as the son of a certain kind of marriage, a travesty of marriage, whose emptiness and meaninglessness are expressed in the person of Linton himself. His superciliousness is encouraged by Heathcliff who, in consistency with his caricature of a marriage, wants to turn his son into the caricature of a gentleman: '"I've ordered Hareton to obey him: and in fact, I've arranged every thing with a view to preserve the superior and the gentleman in him, above his associates"'

(p. 243). Linton is intended to have all the outward appearance of gentility; but without a single trace of noble feeling. His most characteristic qualities of weakness and listlessness are forever being contrasted with the liveliness of Catherine. Her vigour is such that 'she couldn't be still a minute' (p. 234); she bounds around 'like a young greyhound' (p. 247) and is like 'a wild rose' (p. 247) to look at. She is interested in the kind of pursuits which had characterized her mother's attachment to the moors: '"So make haste, Ellen!" she cried, "I know where I wish to go; where a colony of moor-game are settled; I want to see whether they have made their nests yet"' (pp. 246–7). When Heathcliff suggests that they both go out to look for something like a weasel's nest, the young lady from the Grange is 'eager to be active', while Linton shows a shrinking 'reluctance to move' (p. 251). Their separate ideas of heaven both have a natural setting, but Catherine's involves an active communion with nature in motion, whereas Linton has his heart set on inactivity, anaesthesia almost.

The difference between them is sharply drawn in connection with the love letters. When Nelly starts to burn the letters from Linton, Catherine tries to save them by thrusting her hand into the fire, showing the same kind of physical recklessness for the sake of love that had animated her mother. Linton comments on his own part in the epistolary romance in terms which stress his languid self-centredness: '"You should have come instead of writing. It tired me dreadfully, writing those long letters"' (p. 270). Catherine's lack of selfishness is her most positive quality. It is most frequently expressed in her compassion for Linton; she cries on his behalf rather than for her own sake and tells Nelly that she loves him better than she loves herself. Her loyalty undergoes severe trials but remains undimmed. Even when Linton taunts her with the claim that her mother had loved Heathcliff more than Edgar, she forgives him. Her immediate reaction is to upset him from his chair, but she quickly regrets the amount of suffering this seems to cause. It is obvious to the reader that Linton's anguish is assumed – 'He sighed and moaned *like* one under great suffering' (p. 272, my emphasis) – whereas her remorse is genuine and extreme: '"I'm sorry I hurt you, Linton!" she said at length, racked beyond endurance' (p. 272). Linton clearly enjoys making her suffer and he keeps his performance going for as long as possible, eventually relenting (as Nelly observes) 'from lack of breath, by no means from compunction at distressing her' (p. 273). Malice and cruelty are the only things that bring him alive; he turns his destructive energy – the only sort he is capable of – against Catherine, Hareton and (according to Heathcliff) anyone or anything incapable of retaliation: '"Linton can play the little tyrant well. He'll undertake to torture any number of cats if their teeth be drawn, and their claws pared"' (p. 306).

How is it that Catherine develops such a fondness for Linton? At the crucial stage, her 'love' for him is conceived through the medium of letters. In other words, it depends on an ignorance of his real nature. It is worth recalling that Isabella's passion for Heathcliff and Lockwood's would-be philandering are also conditioned by images of the beloved derived from writing. As a matter of fact, the two young people are most comfortable together when they substitute fiction for reality. Linton's chief source of comfort is in listening to the ballads that Catherine recites for him. She does this in a way that reminds him of his mother, and it is an important aspect of their relationship that she often treats him as if he were her child. Their 'love' is carried as far as it is because it resembles the closeness of mother and child rather than that of two lovers: Catherine speaks of herself as a 'woman' and of Linton as her 'pet'. It is significant that he shrinks even from a game of blind-man's buff which, although childish in itself, is symbolic of passion. Unlike her own mother, who had behaved so casually towards Hareton as a child, Catherine's maternal instinct is strong. She does not only mother Linton, but also her father and her own nurse. At one stage, when all of them are ill, she is mothering three people by turns.

Linton's resemblance to Edgar, although superficial, is strong enough to bind Catherine more closely to him. Nevertheless, she has other affiliations much more radical than those that bind her to Linton:

From dinner to tea she would lie in her breeze-rocked cradle, doing nothing except singing old songs – my nursery lore – to herself, or watching the birds, joint tenants, feed and entice their young ones to fly, or nesting with closed lids, half thinking, half dreaming, happier than words can express. (p. 263)

Here, Catherine is seen as a child of nature which provides her with a cradle and which she shares with the birds; at the same time, she is the product of a world which defines relationships in terms of property – the most natural beings are simultaneously 'joint tenants'. The description is a companion piece to Nelly's characterization of Hareton; both of them are in a half-and-half state which will only be transformed into wholeness by their union.

Directly after this description, Catherine crosses the threshold of the Grange. She does this by clambering over the wall surrounding its park rather than by issuing from the door close by: in other words she takes the 'natural' rather than the 'cultural' route out of Thrushcross Grange, and this is symbolic of the kind of compromise she will have to make with the world of the Heights. On the further side of the door, which proves to be locked, she encounters Heathcliff, who plants in her the idea (that Linton is ill) which draws her irresistibly to the Heights. Nelly manages to break the lock and recapture Catherine, for the time being. But from this point on the lock is, in a sense, never secure – the 'cultural' barrier is down and Catherine starts to come to terms with the naturalness partly embodied in Hareton.

It is curious that she begins her civilizing mission with the wrong person – Michael, the stable boy at the Grange. Nelly surprises her one night returning from a clandestine visit to the Heights and forces her to give an account of herself. Catherine, taken off guard by what Nelly aptly describes as her 'espionage', and put to shame by Nelly's rather hypocritical challenge – ' "Why should you try to deceive me, by telling a tale? Where have you been? Speak!" ' (p. 278) – does speak. She explains that she has been bribing Michael with books and pictures to get her horse ready every evening. This giving of culture anticipates the change in the character of her relations with Hareton, although educating Michael is only a means to an end. Paradoxically, she reacts with sarcasm to Hareton's first efforts at teaching himself to read. Although he is endeavouring to cross from his world to hers, against all the odds of his upbringing, she retains enough of the viciousness of her class superiority to laugh 'heartily at his failure' (p. 281) and to experience inward contempt. She attributes his mental exertions to vanity, whereas the pragmatic Nelly interprets them as a desire for self-advancement; they are both wrong, since Hareton has started to educate himself purely for Catherine's sake. When she accentuates the disadvantage he is at by bringing 'some of her nicest books' for Linton (who, typically, 'half gets up' to welcome her) Hareton is provoked to lose his temper with them both. He soon repents of this when it stimulates an apoplectic attack in Linton, and is reduced to tears by Catherine's assertions that he should be put in prison and hanged, not from cowardice but from anguish that she should be so venomous towards him. He shows supreme self-control by not reacting in kind to her striking him with a whip.

After this crisis, Linton deteriorates, growing ever more childish and more petulant, and learning to calculate his shrieking and complaining to obtain the best results. Hareton remains ready to make concessions to Catherine, and after the death of Linton, shows a desire to be 'presentable' in her company. When Zillah offers to help him in this, it reminds us of Heathcliff asking Nelly to make him ' "decent" '. With the comparison in our minds, the difference between the two men is brought home in the tentative way that Hareton makes physical contact with

Catherine: 'he put out his hand and stroked one curl, as gently as if it were a bird. He might have stuck a knife into her neck, she started round in such a taking' (p. 327). The contrast between Hareton's instinctive gentleness and Heathcliff's animal heedlessness is pressed home by a reminder of the fact that Heathcliff had actually stuck a knife into the neck of his wife, Isabella. Catherine goes on to isolate her main ground of complaint against Hareton as his 'disagreeable voice' (p. 328); the fact that what is 'disagreeable' in him is not a personal quality but a social imposition leaves significant room for manoeuvre.

Accordingly, the weakening of her resistance to Hareton is signalled by the introduction of compromising elements in her own language:

'I should like to be riding Minny down there! I should like to be climbing up there – Oh! I'm tired – I'm *stalled*, Hareton!' (p. 331)

She uses Hareton's own language, but she uses his language without thinking, and in the very next minute tries to fight her emerging feelings with an attack upon his '"vile mistakes and mispronunciations"' (p. 332). She challenges him to make a fool of himself by repeating the ballad 'Chevy Chase', but there is an almost willed obtuseness in the specificity of her complaint to Lockwood that '"he has selected my favourite pieces that I love the most to repeat, as if out of deliberate malice!"' (p. 333).

Her spitefulness drives Hareton back into himself, resigning the responsibility for any improvement in their relationship. It is Catherine's turn to make the overtures – their concessions have to be mutual in order to mean anything. After trying to shame him out of his lack of culture by stressing his animality, she eventually humbles herself. But what really reconciles them to each other is a kiss: a spontaneous physical gesture of the kind that Lockwood (and indeed any member of his class) could never perform. What is revealing in Nelly's account of the aftermath of this kiss is a cooperation with the tones and values of Lockwood's language: 'I did not doubt the treaty had been ratified, on both sides, and the enemies were, thenceforth, sworn allies' (p. 345). Once again, love between members of different classes is interpreted as the achievement of peace between warring factions, the suspension of violence that is normally taken for granted.

On Lockwood's final visit to the Heights, the change that has taken place within its walls is immediately suggested by its outward aspect, which is inviting for the first time. Instead of the harsh 'wuthering' wind there is a gentle breeze: 'a fragrance of stocks and wall flowers, wafted on the air, from amongst the homely fruit trees' (p. 338). Here, there is no clash between nature and culture – the fruit trees are 'homely' – and the introduction of garden flowers to the Heights is a significant move; the relationship between Catherine and Hareton depends on a closeness to nature which is *controlled*. Lockwood's first confirmation of the altered state of affairs is the conversation that he overhears between the youthful lovers:

'Con-*trary*!' said a voice, as sweet as a silver bell – 'That for the third time, you dunce! I'm not going to tell you, again – Recollect, or I pull your hair!'

'Contrary, then,' answered another, in deep, but softened tones. 'And now, kiss me, for minding so well.' (p. 338)

In the context of the whole novel, this passage is weighted with irony; for better or worse, the purpose of education, the use of culture, is to bring into line, to translate into its own terms and thus to subdue, whatever is contrary. The love between Catherine and Hareton is more successful and more banal than that of Cathy and Heathcliff in the sense that it can be assimilated to culture – it can be described in a language which everyone understands.

In a way, Hareton learns to read a different meaning in his own name, which is a nature-sounding one (Hare – ton) but which has other, more civil, connotations (Heir – ton). While he and Catherine become more and more domesticated and familiar in style, Heathcliff becomes more and more alien and unassimilable. The superior humanity of the second generation is suggested by the fact that Hareton remains considerate and loyal towards Heathcliff to the end, while Cathy discovers that she is able to forgive him. This undisguised generosity of spirit earns them the right to power and influence, and the novel ends with the prospect of their removal from the Heights to the Grange.

On the face of it, the story ends on a positive note; the love between Catherine and Hareton involves a blending of the opposites of nature and culture, a repairing of those breaches in the fabric of society which had been torn apart by the passion of Cathy and Heathcliff. But it also ends on a muted note; the mood of peace and reconciliation is bought at the cost of losing all the qualities which had seemed to motivate the novel in the first place: the intensity and commitment of the first love relationship and the sheer originality of the experience which had proclaimed its value in its refusal to be extinguished. Are we to regard the final situation of Catherine and Hareton in the light of an enrichment or an impoverishment of their experience? We have to decide what to make of the fact that both Lockwood and Nelly, whom the author has given us plenty of reasons to mistrust, are perfectly in accord with the way that the novel concludes. It may be that the mood of calm and restitution which pervades the last few pages is entirely of the narrators' making, and that the author's point of view, in this as in other matters, is quite different. We will explore the possibilities in the chapter devoted to the ending of the book.

10. Symbolism and Imagery

In my discussion of Catherine's partial emancipation from the values of the Grange, I drew attention to a moment in which she physically crosses its threshold. The symbolic interpretation I gave to this moment was enabled by the knowledge that the text underpins its thematic emphases on division and attempted unity with a series of images of barriers and thresholds. The wall around the park with its useless door is only one such threshold; other walls and doors are similarly referred to, but by far the most significant focus on a barrier between two different states of being is found in the interconnecting references to the image of a window.

Windows have a role to play at most of the important turning-points in the plot. We are first alerted to their importance when Lockwood detects the names scribbled by Cathy on the window-ledge of her bedroom and then when he struggles with the ghost-child who has thrust her arm through one of the panes of glass. As has already been suggested, the fragility of the window represents the flimsiness of the partition which protects a cultivated sensibility from the power of irrational impulses. Lockwood needs to muster all the resources of culture he can lay his hands on – actually a pile of books – in order to expel the awful possibilities he has glimpsed. Heathcliff, however, who has run through all the possibilities of culture during Cathy's lifetime in an attempt to regain his childhood closeness to her, is thrown into despair after her death by a tantalizing sense of her presence at the Heights and on the moors. His only chance of reuniting with her must involve a transgression, not only of the limits of culture but of common definitions of humanity. His attempt to gain access to what lies beyond the grasp of a civilized consciousness involves symbolic gestures like wrenching open the window which Lockwood had noted was 'soldered into the staple' (p. 67).

Nelly's re-creation of the moment when Cathy is first tempted by the spectacle of civilized life at Thrushcross Grange hinges on the barrier of the window through which she and Heathcliff peer. For Cathy, this accentuates her sense of exclusion from the luxury she is drawn to, whereas Heathcliff sees the advantage of staying on the outside. Nevertheless, he threatens that "'if Catherine had wished to return, I intended shattering their great glass panes to a million of fragments, unless they let her out"' (p. 91). Smashing the distinction between nature and culture is precisely what he does do in his subsequent career, when he perverts the system of privileges and exclusions by which culture normally seeks to protect its own. In the meantime, he leaves Wuthering Heights in the belief that Cathy has forsaken him, giving her scope to seal her fate in symbolic fashion when she calls to Nelly to '"shut the window. I'm starving!"' (p. 126).

When Heathcliff returns to the Gimmerton area, Cathy is already married. But her marriage is in a very precarious state; the exact moment of Heathcliff's arrival at the Grange finds her and Edgar seated at a window, hovering, as it were, at the very point of separation between the safe inside and the threatening outside. The view they are looking at has another barrier in it: the ridge of a hill which hides the very real existence of Wuthering Heights. In the crisis which follows Heathcliff's disruption of her marriage, Cathy is heard repeatedly desiring that Nelly should open the window. During her illness, the bouts of delirium in which she imagines herself back at the Heights are punctuated by her frantic appeals to '"Open the window again wide, fasten it open! Quick, why don't you move?"' (p. 163). Quite simply, Cathy needs to break through the barrier which prevents her from joining Heathcliff and the more natural part of existence, in the vague knowledge that the only really effective escape from the Grange will be her own death; appropriately enough, she actually does 'catch her death' through the action of throwing open the window because this brings on a fever which fatally weakens her constitution. Her threat to Edgar that she will kill herself '"by a spring from the window!"' (p. 165) is echoed by her final 'spring' (p. 197) into Heathcliff's arms, after which she never regains consciousness.

Heathcliff is doomed to his human condition, and to separation from Cathy for the rest of his life. While she is released, he is compelled to take his leave of her dead body by climbing in through one of the windows of the Grange. On the evening of the day she is buried, he partially exhumes her grave, and the strain this places on his ability to bear the confinement of mortal life is indicated by the violence with which he re-enters the Heights, smashing down 'the division between two windows' (p. 213).

His final approach to death in graduated stages is accompanied by an increasing eagerness to look out of windows and to lean on window-ledges. Nelly suspects that he has finally given up the ghost when she observes 'the master's window swinging open, and the rain driving straight in' (p. 364). Sure enough, he has died with his hand reaching out of the window, as if in hope of clasping the hand of the ghostly waif:

The lattice, flapping to and fro, had grazed one hand that rested on the sill – no blood trickled from the broken skin, and when I put my fingers to it, I could doubt no more – he was dead and stark! (pp. 364–5)

The scratch on his hand is an echo of the cut wrist of Catherine Linton, and is a means of suggesting that Heathcliff has indeed 'attained his heaven'. Joseph would appear to confirm this, with his conviction that he has seen both Cathy and Heathcliff looking out of the same window 'on every night since his death' (p. 366).

Closely connected with the window motif is a series of prominent references to eyes. Heathcliff's eyes in particular are featured, here in a compound emphasis on both windows and eyes:

'Do you mark those two lines between your eyes, and those thick brows, that instead of rising arched, sink in the middle, and that couple of black fiends, so deeply buried, who never open their windows boldly, but lurk glinting under them, like devil's spies? Wish and learn to smooth away the surly wrinkles, to raise your lids frankly, and change the fiends to confident, innocent angels . . .' (p. 97)

Here, Nelly speaks of something evil, deeply ensconced in Heathcliff, which should make way for an angelic substitute. It is a part of her prescriptions for the change in his outward appearance, a part of the process required to cultivate him. What she assumes to be fiendish is an indication of his true nature, which can only feel restless and out of place in the human condition. Once more, the window represents a barrier between the actual and the potential self.

Heathcliff's eyes, which hold something of a clue to his character, are his most striking feature. At the start of the novel, the first we see of him are his 'black eyes' (p. 45). When he returns from his mysterious absence, his eyes are the means by which Nelly recognizes him. When he is roused to his moment of greatest anger against Isabella, she describes how '"The clouded windows of hell flashed a moment towards me"' (p. 217). This conjunction of the eye motif with the window motif is expressive of Heathcliff's baffled state, in which even continuing to breathe is somehow a falsification of his true nature. His beclouded quality is in striking contrast to the younger Catherine's 'eyes radiant with cloudless pleasure' (p. 247). Her problems require no metaphysical solution, and it is fitting that she should show a facility in gliding in and out of the windows of both Heights and Grange. (Linton, on the other hand, is conspicuously afraid of open windows.) Similarly, Hareton emerges from a Heathcliff-like state when he manages to shake off 'rapidly the clouds of ignorance and degradation' (p. 351). But to return to Heathcliff's eyes: just before his death, they become restless and glittering: 'he had a strange joyful glitter in his eyes, that altered the aspect of his whole face' (p. 357). The altered aspect appears more devilish than ever to Nelly, who tries in vain to make his corpse behave as convention requires:

I hasped the window; I combed his black long hair from his forehead; I tried to close his eyes – to extinguish, if possible, that frightful, life-like gaze of exultation, before any one else beheld it. They would not shut – they seemed to sneer at my attempts, and his parted lips, and sharp, white teeth sneered too! (p. 365)

Nelly closes the bedroom window, but the 'windows' of Heathcliff's eyes will not shut because they symbolize the idea that he has finally crossed the boundary that separates him from his heart's desire.

This tracking of the images of windows and eyes serves to confirm the importance given by the text to the themes of unity and division. The constant emphasis on thresholds is a questioning of the limitations of conventional states of being, which are either broken through completely, as with Cathy and Heathcliff, or made fuzzy and indistinct, as with the second generation. We have to rely to a great extent on the conviction of Heathcliff to believe that Cathy's transcendence of her earthly ties is in fact a fulfilment of her essential nature. He deploys pairs of images which liken her to an unbounded natural force incapable of being contained by domesticity and culture; he says that '"the sea could be as readily contained in that horse-trough"' (p. 186) and that Edgar '"might as well plant an oak in a flower-pot"' (p. 190). However, although it would be slighting to call this wishful thinking, it is among other things a momentary denial of an important part of Cathy which led her to compromise what Heathcliff thinks of as unassailable. We have already seen how her final resting-place seems to partake of both nature and culture at the same time, and it is the unresolved state of this grave which is uppermost in the minds of everyone – narrators, characters and readers alike – as the novel draws to its close.

11. The Ending

The ending of the novel poses a problem for the reader. The cultured way in which Catherine and Hareton resolve their differences, and the social stability which is promised by their marriage and removal to the Grange is a demonstration of how to cope with the problems of yearning and alienation which had turned out so destructively for the first generation. The reader's interest in the power and uniqueness of Cathy's fatal alliance with Heathcliff is meant to be deflected by the complacent tone with which Nelly frames her narrative and by Lockwood's assurance that the dead are at peace. However, it is by no means certain that they are at peace, at least in the sense that they continue to trouble the contentment and worry the nerves of characters and narrators, Lockwood included. And if this means that the movement of the first part of the book is not totally reversed but carries on in a form which cannot be embraced by the reasoned securities of Catherine and Hareton, then the ending of the novel means at least two things at once.

What is the evidence for supposing that Cathy and Heathcliff cannot be repressed, that they survive, either as ghosts or as shadows on the lives of the other characters? To begin with, the rumours are rife: 'the country folks, if you asked them, would swear on the Bible that he *walks*. There are those who speak to having met him near the church, and on the moor, and even within this house – Idle tales, you'll say, and so say I' (p. 366). Perhaps these 'sightings' are no less than should be expected in a small, isolated community for whom the death of its most notorious resident would breed all kinds of speculation. However, Nelly's own unease can be detected in her scandalized emphasis, and in the alacrity with which she turns her back on this vulgar superstitiousness to side with Lockwood's point of view. The 'idle tales' are fairly predictable; Joseph's much more specific witnessing of both Cathy and Heathcliff 'looking out of his chamber window' is less easy to shrug off. Even more peculiar is the little shepherd boy's encounter with '"Heathcliff, and a woman, yonder, under t'Nab,"' (p. 366). The genuine distress of the child, his innocence, and the sixth sense which holds back his sheep, are difficult to explain away, as Nelly discovers when her attempt to do so kindles her own fears:

He probably raised the phantoms from thinking, as he traversed the moors alone, on the nonsense he had heard his parents and companions repeat – yet still, I don't like being out in the dark, now – and I don't like being left by myself in this grim house – I cannot help it, I shall be glad when they leave it, and shift to the Grange!

'They are going to the Grange then?' I said.

'Yes,' answered Mrs Dean, 'as soon as they are married; and that will be on New Year's day.'

'And who will live here then?'

'Why, Joseph will take care of the house, and, perhaps, a lad to keep him company. They will live in the kitchen, and the rest will be shut up.'

'For the use of such ghosts as choose to inhabit it,' I observed.

'No, Mr Lockwood,' said Nelly, shaking her head. 'I believe the dead are at peace, but it is not right to speak of them with levity.' (p. 366)

It is clearly an uphill task for Nelly's common sense to dispel her doubts; she can rationalize the superstitions of other people but cannot suppress her own jitters. The haste, and the accompanying physical vehemence, with which she tries to undo the bad effects of Lockwood's words override the categorical tone of her assertion that the dead are at peace. Moreover, the apparent certitude of this is immediately qualified in a way which shows how badly organized are her imaginative defences. And this comes as no surprise – we know that Nelly is more superstitious than she cares to admit, from the many previous occasions on which she has been unnerved by happenings unaccountable in her own rationalizing narration. She has been frequently disturbed by a sense of the unworldly in Heathcliff's appearance, most recently just before and after his death. But her brushes with the supernatural are not confined to this and the occasional deprecation of inhuman behaviour. Although she is credited with more common sense than any of the other characters, she is also the recipient of one of the most mysterious dream-visions in the book. It happens soon after Heathcliff's return, when she finds herself at a point mid-way between Thrushcross Grange and Wuthering Heights. She pauses to rest by a guide-post, which all at once evokes a 'gush' of childhood memories:

I gazed long at the weather-worn block; and, stooping down, perceived a hole near the bottom still full of snail-shells and pebbles, which we were very fond of storing there with more perishable things – and, as fresh as reality, it appeared that I beheld my early playmate seated on the withered turf, his dark, square head bent forward, and his little hand scooping out the earth with a piece of slate.

'Poor Hindley!' I exclaimed, involuntarily.

I started – my bodily eye was cheated into a momentary belief that the child lifted its face and stared straight into mine! It vanished in a twinkling; but, immediately, I felt an irresistible yearning to be at the Heights. Superstition urged me to comply with this impulse – 'Supposing he should be dead!' I thought – 'or should die soon! – supposing it were a sign of death!'

The nearer I got to the house the more agitated I grew, and on catching sight of it, I trembled every limb. The apparition had outstripped me; it stood looking through the gate. That was my first idea on observing an elf-locked, brown-eyed boy setting his ruddy countenance against the bars. Further reflection suggested this must be Hareton, *my* Hareton, not altered greatly since I left him, ten months since. (pp. 147 8)

I quote the passage at some length to demonstrate not only Nelly's superstitiousness, which is patent, but also the extraordinary palpability of the dream, or apparition, or whatever it is. In Nelly's apt description, it appears 'as fresh as reality', and although her mind is working overtime – tacking between superstition, observation, guessing and reflection – she fails to arrive at any conclusion. The incident remains out of the text's normal focus, and we are given no further guidance as to how to make it fit in with the more realistic parts of the narrative. It is one of the 'loose ends' which we cannot ignore when judging the total effect of the novel's ending.

Also hard to discount is the sheer uncanniness of Cathy's anticipation that she will haunt Heathcliff after her death and his corresponding challenge to her to do so. The validity of their belief in the possibility seems to emerge in the hallucinatory experiences which preface Heathcliff's death, and in the manifestation of her presence which is the climax of his visit to her grave. Cathy and Heathcliff are exempt from the ordinary patterns of behaviour of normal human beings, but there are other, and more mysterious, ways in which they appear to disobey the laws of nature. A fairy-tale atmosphere surrounds both of them: we have already noticed how it clings to Cathy, and it thickens during her illness when she seems to possess the power to transport herself in imagination back to the Heights. She views this as a return to her essential nature, and recognizes (correctly) that Nelly is inimical to it. Most of the novel offers us the spectacle of Nelly trying to deal with Cathy and Heathcliff on her own terms, so it is revealing that Cathy here reverses the operation, and that her terms are specifically supernatural ones: Nelly is a witch who is '"gathering elf-bolts to hurt our heifers"' (p. 161). Heathcliff's career is even more in line with the conventions of fairy-tales; his origins are utterly mysterious, and his rise in society is left unexplained – it is a transformation as if by magic.

By way of contrast, the fantastic elements of the younger Catherine's childhood, such as her 'fanciful tales', are thoroughly dispelled under the rational guidance of Hareton who 'opens the mysteries' of the Fairy cave. The whole drift of their careers is like a process of natural selection, addressed to problems which admit of a *practical* solution.

Lockwood's evidence, if he cared to bring it forward, is the most unsettling of all. His grappling with the ghostly waif cannot be incorporated into a realistic interpretation of events, whether we decide to call it a nightmare or the visitation of a spirit. As Nelly understands it, he is amused by the talk of ghosts, but has she understood right? The fact that she attributes 'levity' to him may only mean that his bearing is more sophisticated than hers. What he actually supposes is that the Heights will now be available

'For the use of such ghosts as choose to inhabit it,' I observed.

At the least, this is an ambiguous remark; we know that Lockwood has actually *seen* some sort of ghost at the Heights (as the visual overtone of his speech attribution – 'I observed' – helps to suggest). He cannot simply have forgotten his terrifying experience; perhaps his attempt at black humour is a form of self-protection.

But what of his closing remarks, which are usually interpreted as a reassurance that the dead are at peace? Notice how Emily Brontë has arranged the syntax and punctuation of the final paragraph to convey the remains of a mood of suspense:

I sought, and soon discovered, the three head-stones on the slope next the moor – the middle one, grey, and half buried in heath – Edgar Linton's only harmonized by the turf and moss, creeping up its foot – Heathcliff's still bare.

I lingered round them under that benign sky; watched the moths fluttering among the heath and hare-bells; listened to the soft wind breathing through the grass; and wondered how anyone could ever imagine unquiet slumbers, for the sleepers in that quiet earth. (p. 367)

This reads like wishful thinking rather than confident relief. Notice how long Lockwood has to 'linger' to make sure that everything is all right; notice how intently he watches for the smallest movement, and how carefully he listens for the slightest sound. He is actively searching for a reassuring image; he needs to create a memory of peacefulness to take away in order to stop himself worrying about the alternative possibility. I am inclined to believe that Lockwood does not really believe that the dead are at peace, and that his closing remarks only reveal his anxiety not to think otherwise.

In any event, much depends on what we take Emily Brontë's attitude to be towards the second generation. And in this connection, I would draw attention to another paragraph on the last page which usually escapes comment. Lockwood has just grumbled about the fact that

Catherine and Hareton seem to be proof against the visit of any ghost (which suggests that he isn't):

> As they stepped onto the door-stones, and halted to take a last look at the moon, or, more correctly, at each other, by her light, I felt irresistibly impelled to escape them again; and, pressing a remembrance into the hand of Mrs Dean, and disregarding her expostulations at my rudeness, I vanished through the kitchen, as they opened the house-door, and so, should have confirmed Joseph in his opinion of his fellow-servant's gay indiscretions, had he not, fortunately, recognized me for a respectable character, by the sweet ring of a sovereign at his feet. (p. 367)

There is a delicate but firm irony at work here. On the very last page of the novel, Brontë chooses to show us how the values of Thrushcross Grange remain unaltered. Money still gives respectability, and respectability hypocritically disguises its real source by a language which gives it a more human face than it actually has (Lockwood leaves Nelly with a *remembrance* rather than a pay-off). The language is as evasive as Lockwood's attempt to make a physical escape. And this in itself is enough to tell us that in spite of the social optimism in the tone of the narrative, the hard facts of social inequality remain exactly the same. The fact that Catherine and Hareton are on their way to the Grange proves only that the Grange has managed at last to take from the Heights what it can make use of, leaving the rest to decay. No wonder that Lockwood is so anxious to lay to rest the spirits of those whose lives partly, and whose deaths wholly, refused even to come to terms with the organized dissimulation that is trying to have the final say.

12. Critical Responses

The history of reactions to the novel is an extraordinarily chequered one. The first critics of the book reviled it – 'we know nothing in the whole range of our fictitious literature which presents such shocking pictures of the worst forms of humanity'[32] – and the element of moral opprobrium is still present in some of the most important modern attempts to establish the present status of *Wuthering Heights* as a 'classic' of English literature.

The first wave of attacks against the novel stressed its potential to deprave and corrupt, singling out the figure of Heathcliff as an example of almost inconceivable viciousness. Certain of the detractors were prepared to admit the originality of the conception and the raw power of its execution, but they were just as often quick to observe that it was a shapeless and 'inartistic' story. The writer was felt to lack skill and judgement, and one result was that Heathcliff was a character difficult to believe in. Nevertheless, the reviewer for the *Examiner* evidently found him a familiar enough type to bear comparison with a Byronic hero like the Corsair, who was 'Linked to one virtue and a thousand crimes'. Elizabeth Rigby, writing for the conservative *Quarterly Review* was concerned to expose the threat of a more than Byronic subversiveness; she found *Wuthering Heights* (and *Jane Eyre*, which she damned in the same terms) politically as well as morally dangerous, and thought that she detected in both books the same revolutionary strain of thought that was producing agitation in England and violent insurrection all over Europe during 1848.

Much less excitable was the reviewer for the *Britannia*, who did not give Heathcliff a Byronic pedigree, but a Wordsworthian one: quoting the poet's dictum 'The child is father of the man', the anonymous critic sought to explain the formation of Heathcliff's violent disposition, instead of simply deploring the end result. Unfortunately, he could not discern the author's purpose in making Heathcliff's vices so prominent, and in this he was not far from the view of Charlotte Brontë, who confided in a letter to W. S. Williams that while she understood the basis of Heathcliff's wickedness, she was sorry that his 'spirit seems breathed through the whole narrative in which he figures'. Charlotte never overcame her unease at the extremism of *Wuthering Heights*, which is probably why she tried to suggest in her 1850 Preface to the book that

Emily was in the grip of something she could not fully understand and could not properly control when engaged in the creation of 'things like Heathcliff'.

It was in response to Charlotte's edition of 1850 that G. H. Lewes composed the most temperate and most astute of the nineteenth-century reviews of the book. He did not praise it unreservedly, but swam against the tide of critical opinion with his recognition of its authenticity and relevance:

The visions of madness are not more savage, or more remote from ordinary life. The error committed is an error in art – the excessive predominance of shadows darkening the picture. One cannot dine off condiments, nor sup off horrors without an indigestion.

And yet, although there is a want of air and light in the picture we cannot deny its truth; sombre, rude, brutal, yet true. The fierce ungoverned instincts of powerful organizations, bred up amidst violence, revolt, and moral apathy, are here seen in operation; such brutes we should all be, or the most of us, were our lives as insubordinate to law; were our affections and sympathies as little cultivated, our imaginations as undirected. And herein lies the moral of the book, though most people will fail to draw the moral from very irritation at it.[33]

For the rest of the nineteenth century, most of the book's readers failed to draw the moral, and were indeed prone to irritation. Leslie Stephen's assessment, in the *Cornhill Magazine* for December 1877, is a typically wincing performance which finds 'even more pain than pleasure or profit in the book'.

It was not until the publication of David Cecil's essay in his collection *Early Victorian Novelists* (1934) that modern criticism was finally diverted from the fixation on questions of taste and propriety that had limited the earlier accounts, and was ready to begin making sense of the book on its own terms. Cecil's main contribution was to divide the characters of the book into two main groups: children of the calm and children of the storm. Calm and storm were opposing principles found in man and nature alike which were independent of any moral categorizations. As well as perceiving that the novel was constructed on a tension of this kind, Cecil took care to explain how its division into two parts was for the sake of reinforcing a pattern. Alluding to the intricate calculations of C. P. Sanger's essay 'The Structure of *Wuthering Heights*' (1926), which was mainly concerned to establish the chronology of the book and the accuracy of its knowledge of legal processes, Cecil managed to disprove the idea that it was an 'inartistic' work, lacking in clear organization. By suggesting a definition of Brontë's outlook as 'pre-moral' rather than 'immoral', he focused attention on the originality of her thinking. However, he started a false trail of his own in trying to insist on Brontë's complete indifference to the social reality of her time: 'she sees human beings,' he says, 'not as [the other Victorian novelists] do in relation to other human beings, or to human civilizations and societies and codes of conduct, but only in relation to the cosmic scheme of which they form a part'.

Somewhat in keeping with Cecil's emphasis on opposing principles of calm and storm, but much more sophisticated, is Dorothy Van Ghent's analysis of the novel in her book *The English Novel: Form and Function* (1953). Her essay on *Wuthering Heights* contains one of the most authoritative readings of the book. She gives a Freudian inflection to the idea that the text operates through a tension between two kinds of reality: 'the raw, inhuman reality of anonymous natural energies, and the restrictive reality of civilized habits, manners, and codes'. Her characterization of these two modes of being is detailed and persuasive and involves an extensive exploration of the imagery of the book; in particular, she provides an extensive discussion of the window motif. But she fails to confront the specifically social context in which what she calls the 'impulse to excess' is set against the 'impulse of limitation'. She tends to dissolve the concreteness of the characters' problems in the interests of relating them to archetypes. She is right to lay stress on the rigorous correspondence between form and content – in fact, she says the form *is* the content – but surely wrong to suppose that those lines of force which run through both the story and its telling do not also run through 'practical social reality'.

A rival method of interpreting the book has been provided by Marxist-orientated critics. Starting from a strictly sociological standpoint, David Wilson's pioneering essay of 1947, 'Emily Brontë: First of the Moderns', makes the important point that the novel issues from a particular set of historical circumstances. His meticulous research into the social and psychological climate of the West Riding in the first few decades of the nineteenth century should not be ignored by anyone wishing to understand the influences on Emily Brontë and her work. Wilson is rather short on criticism of the text, however, and this lack has had to be supplied in the essays of critics like Arnold Kettle and Raymond Williams, who are both interested in what the latter would call the 'structure of feeling' of the times in which Brontë lived. Kettle (1951) makes a suggestive link between the novel and Romantic poetry opposed to the utilitarian values of early-nineteenth-century society. He proposes that Heathcliff's denunciation of Edgar reveals the insincerity of official modes of thought: 'The words "duty" and "humanity", "pity" and "charity" have precisely the kind of force Blake gives such words in his poetry.' (Kettle is thinking of lines such as, 'Pity would be no more/If we did not make somebody Poor;/And Mercy no more could be/If all were as happy as we'). Edgar's 'pity' and 'charity' are mere camouflage for a commitment to social inequality, and Heathcliff's opposition to this makes him morally *superior* to his enemy. Raymond Williams (1973) also puts Brontë in company with Blake, and argues that her response to the human crisis of Victorian capitalism is to place an absolute value on the love of one human being for another. This, he says, 'is to clash as sharply with the emerging system, the emerging priorities, as in any assault on material poverty'. Both Kettle and Williams go too far, it seems to me, in trying to *humanize* the relationship of Cathy and Heathcliff, and in this their analyses seem less well judged than that of Terry Eagleton, whose chapter on Emily Brontë in his book *Myths of Power: A Marxist Study of the Brontës* (1975) offers the most cogent account of the novel so far. Eagleton draws the conclusion that Heathcliff's aggressiveness towards both the old yeoman class of the Earnshaws and the agrarian capitalist class of the Lintons is obliquely symbolic of the role of the industrial bourgeoisie. However, since Heathcliff is also meant to represent the victims of an inhumane society, his position has no precise historical equivalent. He cannot overthrow the existing order without making use of its structures of power. And this is his personal tragedy: he is an embodiment of 'a conflictive unity of spiritual rejection and social integration'. His challenge to the existing order is either distorted by his entry into it, or becomes obscured and meaningless by his refusal to accept the limits of self-definition imposed on him.

Two other approaches to the text, which are completely at variance with each other, are found in the essay by Q. D. Leavis entitled 'A Fresh Approach to *Wuthering Heights*' (1969) and the chapter devoted to the novel in Frank Kermode's book *The Classic* (1975). Leavis takes a highly selective view of the novel, giving first place to the idea that the standards of behaviour of the second generation are an improvement on those of the first. She tends to endorse the judgements of Nelly Dean and even finds Joseph praiseworthy. The main drawback of her scrutiny of the text is its willingness to suppress inconvenient material: the dynamic of the Cathy–Heathcliff relationship is dismissed as incoherent and taken as evidence that Brontë has worked out certain parts of her novel better than others. Leavis's decision to narrow the scope of possible interpretations of the text is reversed by Kermode's emphasis on its openendedness. He takes issue with Leavis, not in order to reject what she has to say, but in order to avail himself of what she wants to reject. His view 'supposes that the reader's share in the novel is not so much a matter of knowing, by heroic efforts of intelligence and divination, what Emily Brontë really meant – knowing it, quite in the manner of Schleiermacher, better than she did – as of responding creatively to indeterminacies of meaning inherent in the text and possibly enlarged by the action of time'. What Kermode is driving at is the probability that the book will mean different things to different readers; and the extent to which this is the case is an index not of its lack of focus but of its built-in productiveness – its ability, in fact, to be a 'classic'. In shifting attention away from the moment of the book's production – which is what the Marxists concentrate on – to the moment of its reception, Kermode is following the example of Emily Brontë herself, inasmuch as she has provided a variety of interpretations in the several accounts of the narrators of *Wuthering Heights*.

The best illustration of Kermode's thesis is the response of contemporary feminist criticism to Emily Brontë's life and work. I have referred more than once to what strikes me as the most impressive example of this school of thought: the analysis provided by Sandra M. Gilbert and Susan Gubar in their book *The Madwoman in the Attic: the Woman Writer and the Nineteenth Century Literary Imagination* (1974). On the one hand, their concentration on a specifically female dimension of experience reveals much more about the sexual aspect of Cathy's struggle for identity than other readers have previously suspected. On the other hand, their understandably insistent focus on female characters tends to reduce Heathcliff to the function of merely duplicating Cathy's desires. His adversarial characteristics even qualify him as 'female' in their eyes. Another critic, Patricia Meyer Spacks (1976), goes further when she defines him as a 'creation' of Cathy's imagination: 'if he were not there, she would have to invent him. In fact, she *does* invent him, directly and indirectly shaping his being.' One can see the point behind all these contentions, while remaining aware of the polemical motive which leads to overstatement. Paradoxically, many of the most telling insights of feminist criticism come from an alertness to the *understatements* of Brontë's writing. For example, Gilbert and Gubar note that on the night Heathcliff elopes with Isabella, he hangs her pet springer from a 'bridle hook'; this combination of circumstances inspires their observation that 'the *bridle* or *bridal hook* is an apt, punning metaphor for the institution of marriage'. This kind of acuity owes a great deal to post-structuralist methods of reading concerned to expose the anomalies of the text, those features of its language which resist being absorbed into the patterns imposed by a conventional reading. The most instructive combinations of post-structuralist method, awareness of sexual politics and Marxist affiliations are the 1976 essay by David Musselwhite I have already made use of and James Kavanagh's 1985 volume on Emily Brontë in the 'Rereading Literature' series edited by Terry Eagleton. Both writers identify the elements of opposition to the attempts of Lockwood and Nelly to exert an ideological control over the material of their narratives. They explain how and suggest why the centrality of the issue of linguistic control has been avoided by traditional criticism, whose genealogical tables of the Earnshaws and Lintons are bound not to include Nelly and Lockwood, possibly because the prejudicial character of the narrator's role is uncomfortably close to that of the critics themselves. Musselwhite's concise essay (which should have been longer) hinges on Lockwood's discovery of Cathy's annotations to the 'legitimate' text, whereas Kavanagh delivers an extensive exposé of Nelly's manipulations. Interestingly, Kavanagh covers much of the same ground as James Hafley's notorious essay of 1958 which identifies Nelly as the villain of the piece. Kavanagh's analysis is sophisticated and scrupulous; but Hafley's condemnation of Nelly, although it has almost always been laughed at for the simplicity of its value judgements, is by no means negligible. Hardly anyone has considered the usefulness of the evidence it brings forward, and in spite of the ham-fistedness of his conclusions, Hafley's basic notions are far less egregious than the vapid metaphysical speculating which has become an almost respectable part of *Wuthering Heights* criticism.

On this note, it would be as well to caution the reader that the critical and biographical literature on Emily Brontë has included more than the usual share of distortions (some of them wilful), guesswork, vagueness and irrelevance. Anyone seeking a reliable guide to the facts that can be distinguished from the fancies, and a solid assessment of the available evidence, is advised to consult the work of Tom Winnifrith; particularly *The Brontës and their Background: Romance and Reality* (1973) and the new biography by Edward Chitham, *A Life of Emily Brontë* (1987).

Appendix: The Poems of Emily Brontë

Emily Brontë was a poet before she was a novelist. Indeed, she might never have become a novelist, but for the chance discovery of her poems which led her sister Charlotte to consider the possibility of all the 'Bell brothers' becoming published authors. At that stage, Emily had already started to collect her verse into two separate notebooks: one devoted to 'Gondal' poems, and the other reserved for more 'personal' compositions. As a matter of fact, the poems of both notebooks are remarkably uniform in character and achievement, and there is very little that distinguishes Gondal poems from non-Gondal ones, apart from specific references to characters and places. The Gondal poems have been prised loose of their original context, and we do not now know how much of a framework Emily or Anne, or both of them, may have provided in the form of a prose narrative. Attempts have been made to reconstruct the outline of the Gondal story – most fully by Fannie Elizabeth Ratchford in her book *Gondal's Queen* (1955) – but there is nothing to authorize such attempts beyond inspired guesswork, and the reader must not expect to learn anything about the genesis of Brontë's narrative technique from a study of her verse. Viewing the poems as individual compositions enables the reader to concentrate on other aspects, such as thematic emphases, settings, moods and predominant ideas. As more than one critic has noted, there is very little development in the verse, which was written during a period of more than ten years; however, there is an augmenting of certain preoccupations. For the reader of *Wuthering Heights*, there are parallels of incident and situation between the novel and the poems, besides the more important correspondences of attitude and thought.

Inevitably, many of the poems evince a love of moorland scenery and of wild weather. The poem beginning with the line 'Loud without the wind was roaring' is typical in its preference for the exhilarating and rugged over the mild and picturesque: 'lovelier than cornfields', for example, are the heather slopes where 'the north wind is raving'. In other poems, the recklessness of natural forces is directly linked with the urgency of man's spirit in its search for freedom, but the single-mindedness of such an approach is not invariable in the poems which grow out of the poet's response to nature. More interesting, perhaps, are those which turn to account the opposing qualities of smoothness

110

and turbulence in nature, in the process of reflecting on a conflict of interests within the self.

Nature often arises in the poems as an object of longing: homesickness for a familiar natural spot becomes almost a routine sentiment, although it is always liable to arresting statement, as in the relatively well-known poem beginning 'A little while, a little while/ The noisy crowd are barred away', in which Brontë is seen using an hour's respite from her teaching duties at Law Hill to return in imagination to the moors around Haworth. The poems of homesickness, of alienation from a beloved place, are closely connected with a much larger group of poems centred on the problems of separation from a beloved person. In many cases, the beloved is separated by distance, as on those occasions when Brontë is deprived of the company of her brother and sisters; but in many more cases, the beloved is separated by death. In the Gondal poems, the speaker is unbearably separated from a lover, while in the non-Gondal poems, the lover is replaced by a kindred spirit with whom the relationship is at once intense and indeterminate. In the Gondal poems of separation, therefore, the situation, range of thought and even range of expression are often conventional – but not exclusively so: one particular oddity is the poem beginning 'In the same place, when Nature wore/The same celestial glow,/I'm sure I've seen these forms before/But many springs ago.' In it, the speaker observes a pair of children who remind her of another pair of children from an earlier generation whose story had been one of separation by death. At least one critic has seen in this a foreshadowing of the second generation aspect of *Wuthering Heights*.

A further inflection of the separation theme explores the viewpoint of the prisoner. Literal imprisonment involves separation from one's loved ones, relatives and friends, while metaphorical imprisonment means being debarred from a wished-for state of mind, or desired state of being. In so far as it excludes one from the ordinary business of mankind, it is never deplored in the poems. Being unable to take part in common pursuits modulates at some point into contempt for them. The 'world without' is judged to be hopeless as compared to the 'world within' of imagination. What, in ordinary terms, would be viewed as a position of weakness is turned into a position of strength through wilful idiosyncrasy. Several poems are only saved from arrogance or perversity by having their lofty or cynical attitude towards the rest of humanity suddenly undercut by the speaker turning the attack against herself.

Brontë shows a particular interest in rather abstract discussions of vices and failings, and in wondering how far they are irreparable and how much they can be atoned for. She asks us to consider the deaths of unrepentant sinners, and in the Gondal poems occasionally focuses on rather Gothic figures who can only be described through negative comparisons with ordinary human qualities. Several of these figures resemble Heathcliff; one in particular has the 'basilisk' eyes that were to terrify Isabella.

A sense of apartness is perhaps the strongest feature of the entire *œuvre*: not just emotional loneliness or a lack of common cause with others, but a self-conscious defiance of religious and philosophical conventions. In the poems dealing with fictional situations, it sometimes looks like the outcome of rhetorical convention when the speaker supplants religious devotion with the love of another human being. But in the more personal poems whose topic is not a love-relationship, it is easier to recognize the unusual completeness of Brontë's spiritual and intellectual independence:

> The earth that wakes *one* human heart to feeling
> Can centre both the worlds of Heaven and Hell.

This has the note of personal conviction, and the whole poem is for and against the same things as the emotional core of the novel. We should not go too far and suggest that it sounds like something either Cathy or Heathcliff might say, because it lacks the wildness that that would entail. It is revealing, though, that within the body of verse we can find the same apparent division of purpose that the ending of the novel sustains. Against the controlled passion of the poem just quoted, we can set the resignation, or scepticism maybe, of the following lines which speak of the unlikelihood of being able to break the moulds of feeling and thought:

> Only I know, however I frown,
> The same world will go rolling on.

Several of the most ambitious poems echo the dualities of the novel in turning inwards to examine the contradictions of the self. 'The Philosopher', for example, voices a desire for annihilation as the only way of resolving a lifelong search to overcome the feeling of inner division. A number of poems, constructed on ostensibly Shelleyan lines, are concerned with the influence of an external force, which is welcomed because it inspires poetry, but which is also feared because it takes over the self and becomes a part of the self while remaining mysterious and unknown. Even an affirmative lyric like 'No coward soul is mine' – which has often been regarded as Emily Brontë's *credo* – depends for its force on a premise of self-alienation. The poet gives way to a force greater than herself as the only means of approaching wholeness. In the novel, Cathy and Heathcliff achieve wholeness through a much more equal communing of hearts and minds. As Margaret Homans has pointed out, in the course of her discussion of Brontë's poetry: 'The form of the novel is fitted for dispersiveness as the Romantic Lyric is not.'[34] One of the motive forces giving the novel the power that it has must have led Brontë to transpose the inner conflicts of the poetry on to the mutually yearning figures of the lovers. The range and 'dispersiveness' of the novel amplifies the meaning of their deaths beyond what may be compassed by the essentially private resolutions of the poems.

Notes

Full details of books referred to in abbreviated form will be found in the Short Bibliography on p. 116.

The edition of *Wuthering Heights* referred to throughout is that edited by David Daiches and published by Penguin Books, 1965 (reissued in Penguin Classics, 1985).

1. Gaskell, p. 94.
2. Charlotte Brontë, 'The History of the Year, 1829', in *The Professor, Tales from Angria, Emma: a Fragment*, ed. Phyllis Bentley, London and Glasgow, Collins, 1954, pp. 47–8.
3. Charlotte Brontë, 'Biographical Notice of Ellis and Acton Bell', in *Wuthering Heights*, p. 36.
4. Ellen Nussey, 'Reminiscences of Charlotte Brontë', *Scribner's Magazine*, May 1871.
5. Gérin, p. 39.
6. C. K. Shorter, *The Brontës: Lives and Letters*, 2 vols., London, Hodder & Stoughton, 1908, vol. 1, p. 216.
7. Gérin, p. 104.
8. Gaskell, pp. 230–31.
9. Charlotte Brontë, 'Biographical Notice . . .', in *Wuthering Heights*, pp. 30–31.
10. ibid., pp. 34–5.
11. Letter, 21 December 1839, cited in Fanny Elizabeth Ratchford, *The Brontës Web of Childhood*, New York, Columbia University Press, 1941, p. 145.
12. Gérin, p. 17.
13. Charlotte Brontë, 'Biographical Notice . .', in *Wuthering Heights*, p. 31.
14. Eagleton, p. 11.
15. cf. Winifred Gérin, 'The Effects of Environment on the Brontë Writings', *Essays by Divers Hands, being the Transactions of the Royal Society of Literature*, New Series, vol. xxxvi, London, Oxford University Press, 1970, pp. 67–83.
16. Margaret Homans, 'Repression and Sublimation of Nature in *Wuthering Heights*', *Proceedings of the Modern Language Association*, vol. 93, 1978, pp. 9–19.
17. Cited in Wilson, pp. 95–6.
18. ibid., p. 96.
19. Charlotte Brontë, 'The Bridal', in *The Professor, Tales from Angria, Emma: a Fragment*, ed. Phyllis Bentley, op. cit., p. 85.
20. Chitham, p. 235.
21. I am indebted for this to David Musselwhite (see Bibliography).

22. ibid.
23. Gilbert and Gubar, pp. 271–3.
24. Holderness, p. 47.
25. cf. Eagleton, pp. 101–2.
26. Bersani, chapter 7, 'Desire and Metamorphosis'.
27. Gilbert and Gubar, pp. 269–70.
28. Kermode, pp. 123–4.
29. Chitham, p. 198.
30. Kermode, p. 122.
31. Kavanagh, p. 91.
32. Unsigned review, *Atlas*, 22 January 1848, p. 59.
33. Unsigned review, *Leader*, 28 December 1850, p. 953.
34. Homans, p. 130

Short Bibliography

Biographical

Chitham, Edward, *A Life of Emily Brontë*, Oxford, Basil Blackwell, 1987.

Gaskell, Elizabeth, *The Life of Charlotte Brontë*, Penguin Books, 1975.

Gérin, Winifred, *Emily Brontë*, Oxford, Oxford University Press, 1967.

Critical

Allott, Miriam, ed., *The Brontës: The Critical Heritage*, London, Macmillan, 1970.

Bersani, Leo, *A Future for Astyanax: Character and Desire in Literature*, London, Marion Boyars, 1978.

Eagleton, Terry, *Myths of Power: A Marxist Study of the Brontës*, London, Macmillan, 1975.

Gilbert, Sandra M., and Gubar, Susan, *The Madwoman in the Attic: the Woman Writer and the Nineteenth Century Literary Imagination*, New Haven and London, Yale University Press, 1979.

Hafley, James, 'The Villain in *Wuthering Heights*', *Nineteenth Century Fiction* XIII, 3, Dec. 1958, pp. 199–215.

Holderness, Graham, *Wuthering Heights*, Milton Keynes and Philadelphia, Open University Press, 1985.

Homans, Margaret, *Women Writers and Poetic Identity: Dorothy Wordsworth, Emily Brontë, and Emily Dickinson*, Princeton, NJ, Princeton University Press, 1980.

Kettle, Arnold, *An Introduction to the English Novel*, vol. I, London, Hutchinson, 1951.

Kavanagh, James H., *Emily Brontë*, Oxford, Basil Blackwell, 1985.

Kermode, Frank, *The Classic*, London, Faber, 1975.

Leavis, Q. D., *Lectures in America*, London, Chatto & Windus, 1969.

Miller, J. Hillis, *The Disappearance of God: Five Nineteenth Century Writers*, Cambridge, Mass., and London, Harvard University Press, 1975.

Musselwhite, David, '*Wuthering Heights*: The Unacceptable Text', *Literature, Society and the Sociology of Literature*, ed. Francis Barker *et al.*, University of Essex, 1976.

Spacks, Patricia Meyer, *The Female Imagination*, London, Allen & Unwin, 1976.

Stoneman, P.M. 'The Brontës and Death: Alternatives to Revolution', *The Sociology of Literature: 1848*, ed. Francis Barker *et al.*, Colchester, University of Essex, 1976.

Van Ghent, Dorothy. *The English Novel: Form and Function*, New York, Holt, Rinehart & Winston, 1953.

Vogler, Thomas A., ed., *Twentieth Century Interpretations of Wuthering Heights*, Englewood Cliffs, Prentice-Hall, 1968.

Williams, Raymond, *The English Novel from Dickens to Lawrence*, London, Chatto and Windus, 1973.

Wilson, David, 'Emily Brontë: First of the Moderns', *Modern Quarterly Miscellany*, No. 1, 1947.

Winnifrith, Tom, *The Brontës and their Background*: Romance and Reality, London, Macmillan, 1973.

FOR THE BEST IN PAPERBACKS, LOOK FOR THE

In every corner of the world, on every subject under the sun, Penguin represents quality and variety – the very best in publishing today.

For complete information about books available from Penguin – including Pelicans, Puffins, Peregrines and Penguin Classics – and how to order them, write to us at the appropriate address below. Please note that for copyright reasons the selection of books varies from country to country.

In the United Kingdom: For a complete list of books available from Penguin in the U.K., please write to *Dept E.P., Penguin Books Ltd, Harmondsworth, Middlesex, UB7 0DA*

In the United States: For a complete list of books available from Penguin in the U.S., please write to *Dept BA, Penguin, 299 Murray Hill Parkway, East Rutherford, New Jersey 07073*

In Canada: For a complete list of books available from Penguin in Canada, please write to *Penguin Books Canada Ltd, 2801 John Street, Markham, Ontario L3R 1B4*

In Australia: For a complete list of books available from Penguin in Australia, please write to the *Marketing Department, Penguin Books Australia Ltd, P.O. Box 257, Ringwood, Victoria 3134*

In New Zealand: For a complete list of books available from Penguin in New Zealand, please write to the *Marketing Department, Penguin Books (NZ) Ltd, Private Bag, Takapuna, Auckland 9*

In India: For a complete list of books available from Penguin, please write to *Penguin Overseas Ltd, 706 Eros Apartments, 56 Nehru Place, New Delhi, 110019*

In Holland: For a complete list of books available from Penguin in Holland, please write to *Penguin Books Nederland B.V., Postbus 195, NL–1380AD Weesp, Netherlands*

In Germany: For a complete list of books available from Penguin, please write to *Penguin Books Ltd, Friedrichstrasse 10 – 12, D–6000 Frankfurt Main 1, Federal Republic of Germany*

In Spain: For a complete list of books available from Penguin in Spain, please write to *Longman Penguin España, Calle San Nicolas 15, E–28013 Madrid, Spain*